The New You

10 hacks to unlock your emotional intelligence
and overcome anxiety & low self-esteem

LEWIS ALERSON

CONTENTS

Part Three - 10 Life Hacks To A New You

INTRODUCTION

Until very recently, the world has been divided into two kinds of people: those who are smart, and those who aren't. It starts from day one of our life, when proud parents look for signs that we are 'bright', 'clever', or intelligent' as opposed to 'dumb', 'slow', or even 'stupid'. Sometimes these labels stay with us as we grow up, and definitely affect the way we view ourselves and others. You know what I'm talking about, right?

How many times have you heard comments like; "he's really intelligent" or, "she's so smart"? All the time, probably. And we even judge ourselves in those terms, which can have a significant effect on our behavior. Having a high IQ (Intelligence Quotient) is even better, and as a society, we look up to and respect those who are deemed superior to us in that area. Most of your life, you have probably measured how intelligent (or not) you are in relation to others, and will have even felt that you weren't smart enough, or maybe that you were, in fact, a genius!

Being a quick thinker, able to solve complicated problems, possessing the ability to retain large amounts of information, and being good with money are just some of the traits or characteristics of someone that you would probably describe as intelligent. And getting high grades at school or university is a common goal which we have all probably aspired to in the past or ambitions which we feel are important for our children to pursue.

Apart from admiring someone who is rich, or very successful, we tend to view intellectual intelligence as the most important mark of a person; something we respect immensely. Smart people have always been our prototypes - think Pythagoras, Albert Einstein, Nikola Tesla, even Bill Gates, and I can already see your jaw drop in awe. Where would we be now without all of those bright brains, who forged our path throughout history?

That's all well and good. But our intellectual abilities aren't everything. For a long time, psychologists had been looking at how we deal with our emotions and the way in which we relate to others. In the 1990s, a couple of them (Peter Salovey and John Mayer), came up with the idea that there is actually another type of intelligence which covers exactly that, known as Emotional Intelligence, or EI. The idea then became mainstream in the mid-nineties through best-selling books and is now a buzz term, often also referred to as EQ (Emotional Quotient).

People described as having emotional intelligence are more likely to be successful in their relationships, their careers, and their social life in general.

The studies show that those who display such skills are more content in themselves, make great leaders, and are also true team players. They are even less likely to suffer from medical conditions associated with stress such as IBS or even cancer, as well as harmful habits like alcohol abuse and eating disorders. It's now accepted in the sphere of psychology that emotional intelligence is more important than intellectual intelligence, which may leave you scratching your head. Why is being able to deal with your emotions so important?

Just think about that for a second – take your emotional temperature at this moment and choose one word which would best describe how you are feeling: frustrated, tired, angry, sad, depressed, anxious confused, stressed-out, disillusioned, disappointed...? It could be any one of these or more; all feelings which prevent you from enjoying this moment. Wouldn't it be great if you could just take control over these negative emotions rather than them controlling you?

Often, our inability to identify exactly how we feel and to evaluate those emotions objectively prevents us from being able to master them, and even express them. But why has this important aspect of our humanity failed to fall under the radar by scientists for so long, and how useful is it really to us today?

We will take a look at the answers to the first part of the question in Part 1 of the book and then explain how important it is for you to begin to incorporate emotional intelligence more into your daily life. In Part 2 you can learn about how being mentally strong doesn't mean that you are cut off from your emotions, but quite the opposite. Tuning in to how you feel can empower you to be more disciplined and develop greater self-esteem. Part 3 will introduce you to 10 essential hacks to guide you through the process of unlocking your emotional intelligence so that your quality of life improves and you build healthier relationships.

If you are reading this book as a total novice on the subject of emotional intelligence, then you will learn exactly what it is and how you can begin to use it to your advantage.

For those of you who are already familiar with the topic but want to delve deeper into the ways in which it can change every aspect of your life, you've come to the right place.

If you are one of the millions of people who suffer from anxiety and feel unable to handle even the smallest of problems, this book will guide you through easy-to-follow steps to overcome your fears.

And for those of you who never felt 'good enough', or find it difficult to deal with social interaction at work or in your personal life, you will discover the key to unlocking your true potential.

Finally, many of you may just have the wrong idea about emotional intelligence and think that it is the opposite of being tough, thick-skinned, masterful, or even manly. If that's the case, you will be surprised to learn in this book that it isn't about any of that.

What makes the topic of emotional intelligence so appealing is that everyone has it: yes, that's right – you are emotionally intelligent – you just don't know it yet. Now is the time to learn about your ability to identify your emotions and to manage them, as well as the emotions of those around you. In short, it's time to create a new you!

Are you ready to begin?

PART ONE

UNLOCK YOUR
EMOTIONAL INTELLIGENCE

<u>What is emotional intelligence?</u>

That's a good question.

The standard definition used by those 'in the know' is that it is the ability to monitor your own emotions as well as the emotions of others. By being able to distinguish between, and identify different emotions correctly, you can use that information to guide your way of thinking and behaviour and also influence that of others.

Sounds simple, right? So why all the fuss about it?

You know when you are feeling angry or sad, and can come up with a zillion reasons why you are justified in feeling as you do. Maybe your boss didn't listen to your amazing idea for a new software program or your partner has just dumped you. Whatever it is, your emotions are a reaction to a certain situation and they have become dominant. Your boss is a total idiot for not appreciating your efforts and the more you think about that, the angrier you get. Your partner has hurt you deeply and you will never trust anyone ever again!

These are natural reactions and no one is going to deny you your right to feel, but knowing how to handle these emotions before they take over your whole perception of life is the key. Allowing them to fester and grow will cause you to act in ways that may be self-destructive now, not to mention how they will negatively color your worldview in the long run.

It's also usually pretty obvious when someone is annoyed or upset with you, by what they say and the way they behave. You don't need a degree in psychology to work that out. When your partner storms out of the room, clearly they are upset about something you may have said or done. And when your colleague slams the phone down on you, obviously you said something they didn't like. You can't control someone else's behavior, and I wouldn't suggest that anyway. But you can understand that everything we do and say has a knock-on effect on the people around us, either positively or negatively.

Well, experiencing emotions is something that we all do, but the point about emotional intelligence is having the ability to deal with them in a way that isn't detrimental to you or your relationships. It's actually about using certain skills to harness those emotions and to manage them in order to give yourself a more balanced, harmonious life. How do you know someone has emotional intelligence? Think of those people in your circle of friends and family: who do you know that listens to you when you tell them your problems or someone who displays great empathy? How many parents do you associate with who are able to act calmly when their young child is having a tantrum or someone that seems to manage stressful situations very well?

Anyone that you know displaying this kind of behavior is probably emotionally intelligent – they are not dictated to by what is going on around them. Instead, people with this quality are in control of how they feel and understand the impact their emotional response has on others. Those who are highly emotionally intelligent are usually very grounded in the way they act and you wouldn't normally see them having emotional outbursts. This doesn't mean that they don't feel (which of course is impossible as we are all human); it's just that they tend to process their emotions before their emotions overtake them.

Imagine driving down the motorway at a safe speed of 70 mph. You are keeping up with the flow of traffic and not going so slow that you might become a nuisance. The ride is going great and you are enjoying the views while listening to your favorite playlist. All of a sudden, a technical issue arises with your accelerator and you lose all control of it, making your car increase speed at an alarming rate – now you are at 80… 100… 120 mph…!

That's a very scary scenario and even life-threatening. You have no control whatsoever over your vehicle and try desperately to brake, without any response. You are hurtling into the traffic ahead of you and need to swerve in and out erratically to avoid a collision. There's no time to react – your heart rate is up and you cannot think straight. Fear has set in. This is hair-raising stuff!

That's pretty much how our mind and body works when we don't use emotional intelligence. Something triggers our emotional response mechanism, things escalate, we go into panic mode, people around us are affected, and we just can't stop ourselves. Ever felt like that? The 'out of control car' example is something that I'm pretty sure you can relate to, even if the analogy is a little extreme.

How does this relate to emotional intelligence? When we talk about emotional intelligence, we are referring to the ability to understand, use, and manage emotions in positive ways. The outcome of this is less stress, better communication, more empathy for others, and being able to overcome challenges more effectively. It has been shown that people displaying such traits tend to form stronger relationships, have more success in their academic or work life, make better decisions, and feel more fulfilled.

If we break it down, there are five main aspects to emotional intelligence that most psychologists agree on and these are:

1. Self-awareness
This is when you recognize your own emotions and how they affect your thoughts and behavior. You are aware of your strengths and weaknesses, and feel confident about your own abilities. How would you rate yourself in relation to this, on a scale of 1 to 10?

2. Self-management or self-regulation
Once you are aware of your emotions, you can begin to manage them. The ability to control your impulses and behavior means that you make more balanced decisions and are able to follow through on them while being able to adapt with greater flexibility. How well do you feel that you manage your emotions, on a scale of 1 to 10?

3. Empathy
This is a tricky one and is not to be confused with simply being 'sociable'. Empathy is the key here; to understand the feelings, needs, and concerns of others that would otherwise go unnoticed. Picking up on emotional cues and putting oneself in someone else's shoes creates a stronger social dynamic. How much empathy do you feel that you exhibit, on a scale of 1 to 10?

4. Social skills
This aspect of emotional intelligence relates to how well one maintains healthy relationships, communicates clearly, and inspires others to

collaborate successfully. Conflict management also comes under this umbrella and is often equated with those showing great leadership qualities. How good a leader would you say you are, on a scale of 1 to 10?

5. Motivation
Surprisingly enough, being self-motivated is a sign of emotional intelligence. People who are highly motivated approach each goal with greater enthusiasm for a longer duration, and achieve more positive outcomes. Challenges are not seen as something negative during the process, but more of a learning experience. How motivated do you feel about your goals, on a scale of 1 to 10?

Many people may only have one or two of these traits. I have a friend who is extremely motivated, which has led him to enjoy a very successful and rewarding career in investment banking. But when it comes to empathy, he sucks. That's a problem in his personal relationships because it prevents him from really being able to connect with others. You may know someone who seems to be very confident but lacks the ability to communicate their ideas to others, and comes across as cocky.

You will observe some of these qualities in yourself too, and also be aware of your weaknesses. That is absolutely fine. The reason you are here is to learn how to develop your potential for emotional intelligence so that you can find a balance in your life, your relationships, and your goals.

The question is, what evidence is there that emotional intelligence actually exists at all. Could it be that it is just some buzz term or gimmick invented by pseudo-psychologists to sell more books? Your suspicions are understandable, but the truth of the matter is that it is becoming a very exact science as more and more research is carried out on the topic.

The pioneers of the term first introduced their theories in 1990. The highly qualified academics Peter Salovey and John Mayer presented a paper that gave answers to one of those pending questions in the world of psychology – is there another kind of intelligence, apart from the one that is already recognized? Previous theories had been bent on the belief that emotion was a rival to reasoning – a bit like East versus West. What Salovey and Mayer did was to show that emotions could in fact motivate productive outcomes when properly managed.

That's a pretty liberating thing if you think about it: no longer are we to be divided into camps of those who are clever and those who are just over-emotional. And by laying out exactly what this new term means, the two psychologists provided a path through which one can aspire to achieve it.

The strict definition that they gave in their original paper was this: "The ability to recognize, understand, utilize, and regulate emotions effectively in everyday life."

The interest sparked by this new take on how we behave led to a best-selling book by the author and science journalist Daniel Goleman in 1995, who described emotional intelligence in a way that the layperson could understand. Since then, emotional intelligence has been attributed as one of the secrets to success. By teaching it in schools, it is claimed to aid children's learning abilities and help them succeed while eliminating behavioral problems. If we can learn emotional intelligence from a young age, we will become better adults. What's more, it is now recognized as something we can actually learn, and isn't dependent on genetics, unlike many things in life nowadays.

So, can we measure emotional intelligence, or is it just a hunch we have about somebody? Tons of studies have been done on the subject and of course, ways of testing have come under very intense scrutiny. What defines someone as emotionally intelligent and how did they get like that? Are you even a little emotionally intelligent?

Like any good science story, there has been a bit of controversy about the way people are tested for emotional intelligence. You may have done a quiz in a magazine when you were younger, in which you are posed with a possible scenario and had to choose one of four options. Depending on your results, a score at the end of the test would 'tell you' something about your personality or character. While fun to do, these findings aren't always accurate, as I am sure you can imagine. And unlike IQ tests (Intelligence Quotient), which check your cognitive abilities, EQ tests (Emotional Quotient) are a little more complicated. They involve assessing your ability to deal with certain situations and your skill set to solve emotional problems. The belief is that emotional intelligence is a distinct ability that can be measured objectively, rather than by self-assessment, which isn't very reliable.

The results of all of these tests, which have been fine-tuned over time, show that emotional intelligence is a force to be reckoned with. A study on college students in 2019 by Lynda Jiwen Song and colleagues found that, although IQ is closely linked to academic success, it doesn't guarantee an A+ in a student's social life. We already know that just having a high IQ doesn't help you make friends or be more socially adept, while being emotionally intelligent can make up for your bad maths grades. Imagine going for a job interview, ready to show off your long arm of qualifications, but being unable to overcome your nerves, anxiety, and lack of confidence.

Who will employ you?

In 2009, researcher Delphine Nelis posed the question: "How is it possible to increase emotional intelligence?" An experiment was set up to try to answer that, with two groups being tested on EQ; once at the beginning of the study and once at the end. The 'treatment group' received four group training sessions of two hours on EI while the control group received no training at all. The results at the end of the experiment showed that while the control group showed no change, the treatment group showed significant gains in their EQ.

Studies like these paved the way for a lot of innovative work that has subsequently been carried out, all of which goes to show that emotional intelligence is a real factor in our relationships, our mental frame of mind, and our success. And it's attainable!

Most EQ appraisals are based on Goleman's 5-factor structure that we mentioned above, which are:

• Self-Awareness
• Self-Regulation
• Motivation
• Empathy
• Social Skills

Within each category, you can find certain sub-skills and abilities that contribute to even higher emotional intelligence, which we will look at now. As we go through the points, pause for a second at each one and think about how much or little it may relate to you. This isn't a test about how good or bad a person you are; it's just a nudge for you to consider which areas of your life you can improve on. Think of it as a kind of EQ checklist that you can keep coming back to and reflect upon. You may mentally tick off in your mind which qualities you feel you possess, or which ones you would like to improve upon. Emotional intelligence isn't something that you can acquire overnight, so be patient with yourself and trust in the process.

1. Self-Awareness:

- Emotional awareness: recognizing your emotions and their effects
- Accurate self-assessment: knowing your strengths and limits
- Self-confidence: being sure about your self-worth and capabilities

2. Self-Regulation:

- Self-control: managing your disruptive emotions and impulses
- Trustworthiness: maintaining honesty and integrity
- Conscientiousness: taking responsibility for your personal performance
- Adaptability: being flexible when handling change
- Innovativeness: being open to novel ideas and new information

3. Self-Motivation:

- Achievement drive: striving to improve or meet a standard of excellence
- Commitment: aligning with the goals of the group or organization
- Initiative: readiness to act on opportunities
- Optimism: persistence in pursuing goals despite obstacles and setbacks

4. Empathy or Social Awareness:

- Empathy: sensing others' feelings and taking an active interest in their concerns
- Nurturing others: sensing what others need to develop, and supporting their abilities
- Accepting diversity: cultivating opportunities through diverse people
- Listening: Giving the time and space to others to express themselves

5. Social Skills:

- Communication: sending clear messages
- Leadership: inspiring groups and people
- Conflict management: negotiating and resolving disagreements
- Building bonds: nurturing fruitful relationships
- Collaboration and cooperation: working with others toward shared goals

This may seem like a lot to take in, but every point falls within the spectrum of our capabilities. We have the potential for so much more than we are often aware of. Just pondering on some of these aspects will provide you with food for thought about how you normally behave, how you feel, and how you view your place in your social group. You can start by choosing any one of the above pointers and write down how effective you are.

Let's say that you choose Adaptability: being flexible when handling change. Think of the last time in the recent past that you found yourself in a situation where change was inevitable. It may have been when you had to move house or re-position within your job. Try to recall how you felt prior to the change — were you anxious, frustrated, fearful, hesitant? As the change inevitably occurred, did those feelings get stronger? If so, how did you handle the eventual shift in your life? Could you have managed the change with less heart-ache or grief? Could the transition have been made smoother if you had approached it differently?

Only you know the answers to these questions, although you may not be aware of that now. Just going through them in your mind will help you to realize more about yourself and give you greater clarity about how your emotions affected the whole situation. You are one step closer to understanding emotional intelligence!

How can it benefit you in your life?

You probably remember the movie Rain Man, in which Dustin Hoffman portrays the character Raymond Babbitt; a man with savant syndrome. Although a very rare condition, the film brought to light how those with the condition are capable of amazing intellectual feats, such as multiplying and dividing large numbers, remembering what day of the week April 12 fell on in 1927, or able to memorize the complete phone book.

This is an extreme form of 'intellectual activity' which can be associated with autism, developmental disabilities, acquired brain injuries, or injuries to the central nervous system. We often marvel at anyone with such abilities but are also aware that they may be lacking in many attributes that we take for granted, such as social finesse, the ability to live independently and having the necessary life skills to manage everyday practicalities.

You may not know any savants, but you have probably come across a few people who have an extremely high level of intelligence, or just folk who seem pretty smart. The emphasis that we have placed in society on intellectual intelligence up until now is evident wherever you go. No one wants to be considered dumb, slow, or "not too bright". And from our first day at kindergarten, we are constantly being assessed for our mental aptitude and problem-solving abilities. As you worked your way through school and perhaps college, the aim of the game was always to get good grades, right? You were tested and assessed on how much you knew about a particular subject – this was the mark of how "intelligent" you were.

And that still applies in daily life, from "getting it" when presented with new procedures in the workplace, to being able to grasp the latest technology. In fact, we are all still judging ourselves and others based on how much we "know or don't know" about a particular subject. An expert on nuclear physics or digital trends is held up in high esteem because he or she knows a lot of stuff about those topics. But no one has ever been graded or received a Nobel prize for their level of emotional intelligence!

And yet, all of the studies coming out tend to show that it's not the smartest people who are the most successful, but those with greater emotional intelligence. Sure, your IQ can help you get into college, but it's your EQ that is going to help you manage the stress levels when sitting your finals. Having the expertise needed to get you to the top in your chosen career is fine, but it's not going to guarantee you fulfillment on a deeper level. The perfect mix is to be able to use your IQ and EQ in tandem, as the one is not exclusive to the other.

The benefits of developing your emotional intelligence are numerous, so if you are wondering exactly what they are, let's take a look.

Firstly, think about your performance at school or work.

Companies nowadays use a wide range of recruitment techniques to assess the suitability of possible candidates for a specific position. When you apply for your next job, you may be asked to complete one of these 'tests', which can range from knowledge of the job itself to your cognitive abilities. And guess what other kind of test you may be asked to take: an emotional intelligence test!

Your future employer is looking to see how well you build relationships and understand emotions (both your own and those of others around you). These are now seen as important factors in professions that require good interpersonal skills and even reveal leadership qualities.
If you do well in this test, you may stand a better chance of being recruited for the job, even if candidate X has more qualifications than you. Slowly, employers are coming to realize that being emotionally intelligent is just as important, if not more so, than academic achievements.

I recall being at High School and there was a boy in my class who was very popular, even though he certainly wasn't anywhere near an 'A' student when it came to grades. Despite that, he was captain of the soccer team and had a large circle of friends. He was well-liked by the teachers too, who went the extra mile to help him with his physics and maths homework. Eventually, he did manage to pass his end-of-year exams, mostly due to his likeability and the extra encouragement and assistance he got.

You could say that he had a certain degree of emotional intelligence. His interpersonal skills were spot on – he was friendly with everyone, he always encouraged his team's players, and was very respectful of the teachers. All of these factors together enabled him to succeed in the end, and you can understand why.

Secondly, consider your physical health.

When you fail to manage your emotions, you fail to manage your stress levels too. That can have serious consequences for your health. Imagine the scene: you have been waiting in the queue at the supermarket for ten minutes and someone cuts in ahead of you. That's like waving a red flag to a bull for most of us. Before you know it, the indignation causes a stress spike, and your body produces hormones such as adrenaline, which trigger your fight or flight response. This momentary state of fear can make your heart beat more rapidly, which raises your blood pressure. If these spikes happen on a daily basis, they eventually cause damage to your blood vessels, heart, and kidneys. That sounds like a very dangerous over-reaction to someone jumping the queue, right?

Emotional intelligence can prevent you from getting into this state in the first place, once you learn how to use it. Apart from the negative consequences to your body of being in a constant state of fear, stress can also be highly detrimental to your mental wellbeing. When we feel angry at the queue-cutter, we are actually prepping ourselves for anxiety and depression. If you can't deal with your anger, this could eventually prevent you from having enriching relationships, leaving you feeling socially isolated. I'm not saying that you are unjustified in feeling angry when you see someone behaving in a rude or inconsiderate manner. The point is that your emotional response to such a situation can have a very negative outcome on your health further down the road.

The next time you are waiting in a queue and someone cuts in, instead of allowing your anger (and blood pressure) to rise, just let them pass. You have no idea who they are, what problems they may have, and why they are in such a hurry. But at the end of the day, what matters is your wellbeing, and allowing them to step in ahead of you is a really insignificant event in the whole scheme of things.

Thirdly, consider your relationships.

Once you begin to understand your emotions, you are better able to control them. This enables you to express how you feel much more effectively, and also to understand how others feel. When a 2-year-old goes into a full-blown tantrum, that's because a child of that age has neither the verbal skills nor the emotional maturity to express how they feel coherently. There's a very good reason why that stage of development is known as 'the terrible twos'.

As the child grows and becomes more articulate, it is able to express exactly how it feels with the spoken word. But somewhere along the way, we seem to lose that capacity, as society pulls us into a bad habit of keeping our emotions locked down. It is therefore just as hard to understand an adult who doesn't express themselves well as it is understanding a screaming toddler having a tantrum in the middle of the high street.

Many couples facing relationship problems resort to counseling, in which a trained professional acts as a kind of mediator between the two parties. In cases such as this, when communication has completely broken down, the couple finds it extremely hard to express how they feel to each other but may be able to share their thoughts and emotions reasonably well with a third-party. Not dealing with how you feel and pushing it to the background cannot fix a broken relationship, and that applies to all of your relationships – not just with a spouse or partner.

By acquiring the tools of emotional intelligence, you can start to improve existing relationships in the home, at work, with friends, and your extended social circles. They will also enable you to create deeper, more meaningful connections that can bring greater enrichment to your life as a whole.

This brings us to our fourth point, social intelligence.

You don't need to have a large circle of friends to be classed as having social intelligence. It's all about the quality of your relationships, and not the quantity. When you are in tune with your emotions, there is a social consequence to that which can bring you closer to people in your everyday interactions.

Saying good morning to the doorman as you enter the office is not necessarily a life-changing event, but by not saying good morning, you are projecting the image of someone who only cares about him or herself. It doesn't cost anything to be polite, but more than that; you are establishing a friend-friend relationship, as opposed to a foe-foe dynamic. You may even strike up a conversation with said doorman one day and discover that your kids go to the same school, or that you have similar interests.

Feeling that you have an 'ally' instead of a 'hostile enemy' reduces stress, balances your nervous system, and makes you feel happy. No matter how large or small your social circle is, and whether or not you get on with everyone at work, maintaining a balanced connection can seriously benefit your overall wellbeing. Emotional intelligence allows you to attain that, as you come to understand how your words, mood, or behavior can have a positive effect on yourself and those around you.

The late, great Sir Ken Robinson was an innovator in the way we view education and published several books and articles on the subject, as well as giving extremely entertaining TED talks. He focussed on the power of creative and cultural education across the world, aiming to unlock and ignite the creative energy of people and organizations. In one of his much-viewed TED talks entitled 'Do Schools Kill Creativity?' which has been viewed online over 60 million times by an estimated 380 million people in 160 countries, he gets to the bottom of how emotional intelligence, as well as other types of intelligence such as kinetic, have been largely ignored in the educational system.

In the talk, among other things, he discusses how before the nineteenth century there was no public system for education, which all eventually came about to meet the needs of industrialism. Fast-forwarding to today the system of public education around the world is a protracted process of university entrance. The consequence of this is highly talented people think they're not creative because they've gone through a system which devalues creativity and puts academic ability above all else.

As we begin to understand that intellectual intelligence is not everything, the floodgates are starting to open for other kinds of intelligence, and EQ is just one of them. By harnessing the power of how you feel, being able to manage those emotions, and improving your social interaction with others, you are on your way to creating a happier, more fulfilled you.

Understanding your emotions

What are emotions?

Of course, you know the answer to that in basic terms - they are what you feel, right? Most people don't really give much thought to how they arise, what controls them, or their significance in everyday life. As humans, we are all capable of many different kinds of emotions and will actually experience several of them from the moment we wake up till the time we go to sleep. How do you feel at this moment: happy, sad, angry, content, excited, bored?

Depending on who you talk to, there are several theories about how many emotions exist. Going way back to ancient Greece, Aristotle proclaimed that there are nine basic emotions, many of which had an opposite. So, anger had calmness as its counterpart, while shame was the other side of confidence, and so on. He presented a list something like this:

- Anger as opposed to calmness
- Friendship
- Fear as opposed to courage
- Shame as opposed to confidence
- Kindness as opposed to cruelty
- Pity
- Indignation
- Envy or jealousy
- Love

Do you find anything missing in his list? What about hate? How often have you said that you hated this or that? How frequently have you felt hostility towards someone? Do you often feel loved or compassionate? What about pain? Emotions are like keys on a piano - they may be divided into black and white, but when two or more keys are played together, different note combinations produce different sounds – some beautiful and some hard to listen to. Emotions are a complex thing, just like music, which can be felt and expressed in many different ways.

Another list of emotions was set out by Robert Plutchik, who was an emeritus professor at the Albert Einstein College of Medicine and also a professor at the University of South Florida. He's well known for his theory on the eight basic emotions, which are fear, anger, sadness, joy, disgust, surprise, trust and anticipation. You can already see that some are positive emotions, some negative, and some neutral.

Plutchik designed a diagram known as the wheel of emotions, or the

Plutchik Model, which is a bit like a colourful eight-petalled flower. Each petal represents the eight basic emotions and is subdivided into particular traits. One leaf represents acceptance, trust and admiration for example, with love and submission sitting to each side of it. The closer to the centre of the wheel you get, the darker the colour, which represents the intensity of emotions felt.

That's an interesting point because it is basically showing that if we leave our emotions unchecked, they do indeed intensify, which is why understanding them is so important. If you can nip your annoyance in the bud, you avoid it escalating into full-blown anger, so it is a great tool for identifying emotions and seeing how they can develop.

We can understand a lot about how people are feeling just from their facial expressions. Past research has given us a lot of insight into the seven universal facial emotions: anger, contempt, disgust, fear, joy, sadness, and surprise. A study by Wallace V. Friesen and associates of the University of California in 1972 found that the same facial expressions of emotions were produced spontaneously by members of very different cultures in reaction to film that elicited emotions. Any great actor knows that it's all about the face and there is a reason why stage actors wear an enormous amount of make-up to emphasize the eyes and mouth in particular. You may not understand Japanese, but if you watch a Japanese movie, you are very likely to gauge the emotions of the actors in general terms, whether they are feeling sad, surprised or angry.

You can also tell how someone is feeling by studying their body language and emotions like pride, pride, shame, anger, fear, and disgust can be accurately deciphered just by observing nonverbal bodily displays. When you hang your head low, it can also mean dismay, disappointment or weariness, so it very much depends on the context. Take a look around you and see if you can gauge how someone is feeling just by looking at their body language.

We can learn a lot about how someone feels by how they speak. There are literally thousands of semantic cues that express one's emotional state, and that's not just the words we use. Our pitch, loudness and rate of speech are dead giveaways. Imagine an excited child and how quickly they may talk; it is obvious just by the speed at which they speak that they are bubbling over with enthusiasm. Adults do that too, although may try to contain themselves, for whatever reason. But if you listen very carefully the next time someone is talking to you, notice the underlying emotion in their voice from the way they speak, rather than just the words they choose.

Obviously, we do also express how we feel through what we say or don't say, and this is a very important aspect of emotional intelligence. How many times have you vented your frustration to friends, or vocalized your love for someone? It's all part of human interaction and what comes out of our mouth has direct implications on the listener. Think about it: how do you express gratitude? Is it a simple "thank you" or do you articulate how much you appreciate someone's action with words like, "I really appreciate what you have done for me and want to thank you for your kindness"? I think you'll agree that there is a huge difference between the two!

A couple of researchers at the University of Berkeley recently carried out an amazing study on discrete emotions, a bit like the combination of piano keys that I mentioned earlier, and came up with a list of 27 types of emotions experiences. In 2019, Alan S. Cowen and Dacher Keltner used statistical methods to show how many kinds of emotional states can be found within a semantic space by using 2,185 short, emotionally evocative videos.

They came to the conclusion that there are 27 varieties of emotional experience, with clusters of states such as awe, fear, envy and so on. The truth is that often we don't know how we feel, or can't quite put our finger on it, never mind express it. Learning about the many different shades of emotion is one way of being able to define and articulate more clearly exactly how you feel.

Let's take a look at the list and as we do so, pick out one positive emotion that you have experienced yourself in the past week, and one negative one:

1. Admiration
2. Adoration
3. Aesthetic Appreciation
4. Amusement
5. Anger
6. Anxiety
7. Awe
8. Awkwardness
9. Boredom
10. Calmness
11. Confusion
12. Craving
13. Disgust
14. Empathetic pain
15. Entrancement
16. Excitement

17. Fear
18. Horror
19. Interest
20. Joy
21. Nostalgia
22. Relief
23. Romance
24. Sadness
25. Satisfaction
26. Sexual desire
27. Surprise

Which number did you choose from the positive side, and which one from the negative? Thinking about both, what triggered those feelings and how did you deal with them? What was the after-shock of something negative that you felt, and how did that positive emotion affect you, and those around you? I chose number 24, sadness, as a negative, because someone in my extended family recently passed away. I think that I was justified in feeling that and saw it as a natural response to losing a loved one. The feeling lasted for a few days, before gradually fading into a warm sense of nostalgia.

As a positive emotion, I chose number 1, admiration, for a friend of mine. Robert, who has just opened his own gym – a long-time dream of his. It's a good feeling to see him succeed and knowing how much he worked to achieve his goal. My admiration for him will probably stay with me, as well as being an inspiration for my own future ambitions.

Experiencing emotions is part of who we are, and being conscious of both the good and the bad is essential if we want to maintain a healthy balance in our lives. Your outlook on events and people around you today can shape your tomorrow, so getting a handle on that can be the make or break of a full, contented life.

I've mentioned some theories about the many kinds of emotions we experience and ways of identifying them, but you may still be wondering what triggers them. On the surface, it's easy to say that they are a result of someone else's behaviour, or due to a particular event or incident which you may or may not have been personally involved in. Actually, it is us who are responsible for triggering our emotions, and when I say us, I mean our brains.

A lot is going on inside your head that you are most likely completely unaware of, unless you're a neuroscientist! It's a pretty complicated set of wiring that you have up there, and have no doubt about it – your brain is programmed to process every nanosecond of information and external sensory stimuli before you can say "humbug!"

While you are getting riled up because someone just stole your parking spot, the old grey matter has already started interpreting the situation, calculating your options and crafting responses. You may think that emotions are internal states, and that is correct, but it's a bit more complicated than that. Emotions are a mix of cognitions, feelings and actions, which means that they are not only how we "feel", but also how we process and react to those feelings. It is your brain that is doing most of the work.

It is hardwired to evaluate what is going on, and we only need to think of the flight or fight response to understand that. Fear helps us to escape life-threatening situations, and our brain raises the alarm bell after processing the risks. It produces the emotion of fear in order to help you survive. If a rabid dog is chasing you, the fear factor kicks in and you react without seemingly having time to "think" about it – your brain has already done that for you. It sends a signal to your motor-neuron system and pumps adrenaline through your blood, forcing you to leg it, pronto!

Your brain is also the most advanced chemistry lab in existence. Pharmaceutical companies have yet to reproduce anything nearly as sophisticated.

Information travels within the brain via neurons, which are cells that transmit signals through what is known as neurotransmitters. These are chemicals, which aid internal communication in the brain, with the most studied ones being dopamine, serotonin and norepinephrine. Dopamine is the pleasure fixer and is responsible for reward-learning processes. Do something good, and you get a hit of dopamine, which makes you feel a sense of pleasure and happiness. The more you experience this, the more you want it, and your brain gets conditioned to achieving that on repeat.

Serotonin is a neurotransmitter responsible for your memory and how you learn. Studies have shown that it plays an important role in regenerating brain cells and could even ease depression. If you are feeling very low, anxious, or suffering from panic attacks and visit your doctor, he or she will quite possibly issue you with a prescription drug containing serotonin if you fall into the definition of someone suffering from depression. (Such a chemical imbalance can be rectified with the right treatment, but the advice of a health professional is paramount and under no circumstances should you enter into self-diagnosis or take any kind of drug without first seeking medical help.)

Norepinephrine is your mood moderator and helps to control stress and anxiety. If this chemical is out of sync, it can seriously affect how your brain receives and processes it, which can impact your mood enormously. It may prevent you from getting the right shots of dopamine, which could leave you feeling unhappy, even when everything around you is going great. It can also hinder the distribution of serotonin, resulting in depression and other mental illnesses.

Apart from using this arsenal of interactive chemicals, your brain is also using different areas for different emotions. Think of a PC - it is made up of several bits of hardware, such as the CPU, the power unit, and the graphics card, as well as the software to make it functional, all wrapped up in a nice tidy box. Each feature does its bit to run and your brain is no different. The area used to process emotions is known as the limbic system, which includes the amygdala. This almond-shaped mass of cells, or nuclei, lies deep within the brain's temporal lobes and is the traffic control tower of reactions associated with fear, including the fight or flight response.

Your hypothalamus sits just under the thalamus and above the pituitary gland and is a highly specialised part of the brain. Imagine it as the supervisor of a warehouse, responsible for regulating and organising the stock, and keeping tabs on what comes in and what goes out. The hypothalamus does just the same, regulating your emotional response to stimuli. When things are transported from the short-term memory to your long-term memory, it's your hypothalamus that acts as the warehouse overseer, helping you to retrieve stored emotional responses. A feeling of panic on realizing that you are being followed while walking down a dark street, accompanied by a rapid heart rate, a rise in blood pressure and quickening of breath, is all the work of your hypothalamus.

If you are afraid of tarantulas, you may even flee at the sight of a common house spider, because your brain is already on red alert. This is how irrational fear can be, and in the same way, you could equate that with anxiety, stress, anger, feelings of low self-esteem or any other negative emotions which disrupt your wellbeing. Once you understand that, you are in a better position to deal with all of the above.

The funny thing about our brain is that it is a joint partnership – each hemisphere working with each other to try to reach mutual agreements. Each side processes information differently, with the right hemisphere identifying input and the left interpreting it in order to make a logical response. It's a great system, although you need to bear in mind that it is dependent on past experiences, so may not always produce the appropriate response. For example, if your past romantic relationships have ended in betrayal, you will probably find it difficult to place your trust in someone else again because your brain is telling you that this is the norm.

Whenever you recall a negative memory, it will immediately make you feel negative again. On the other hand, recalling happy moments will lift your mood and fill you with optimism. Just bringing up past memories can have a significant effect on your present mood, your decisions and your outlook. So how do you turn that around? By realising that past memories belong exactly there – in the past, and by being conscious of how your thought patterns now are being influenced by an event in your life that is over and done with.

Think of an unpleasant experience that you had in the past. Let's say that you fell off your bike as a kid and broke a leg. Does that mean that you should never ride a bike again? Certainly not, but the memory of the trauma is reinforced every time you think about it and even just seeing a bike may trigger that memory. You also get used to anticipating that fear, which increases the emotional response even more, though rationally speaking, there is no real reason now to be afraid of bikes. This is just our emotions getting the best of us, with our brain doing its job. The point is to see that for what it is, which takes practice.

You may have noticed that most of the emotions I have been using as examples here are negative ones, but positive experiences are also reinforced so, the more you have of them, the better. At the end of the day, the phrase "positive thinking" really can be beneficial, so don't give up just yet!

Men versus women

It's not a competition between the sexes.

We are all capable of emotional intelligence, although historically and culturally speaking, women have been singled out as being more "emotional" than men. How does that sentence make you feel if you are a man? Do you agree or disagree with it? If you are a woman, do you relate to it or have a different experience? Whatever your opinion on the subject, it is worth opening a dialogue about it in relation to emotional intelligence.

In the 1960s, the feminist movement really took off, with books like The Female Eunuch and The Feminine Mystique bringing to the forefront the way women had been perceived up until then in patriarchal societies and thereby discriminated against. Many things have changed since then for the better, especially in legislative terms, in the workplace, the home, in our lifestyle choices and in the way we perceive equality. More recently we have seen the 'Me Too' movement, while men have also won the right to paternity leave to help raise their children in almost all developed countries. And yet, most studies do show that there remains an inconsistency between the way men and women experience and express emotions.

Why is that? And, if it is the case, does it matter? Many of you reading this book, regardless of gender, will have had some experience of sex discrimination or stereotypical expectations. And it works both ways. Men who cry in public may be seen as unmasculine, while women who are very tough are often seen as unfeminine. We are not going to dive into the long-running debate on the differences or similarities between the genders here: that is not the aim of this section.

Instead, it is useful just to take a look at how our ability to attain emotional intelligence may have been hampered by external cultural and societal forces, or even by our own preconceptions about what we can or cannot do. It's time to dispel the myth – we are all capable of emotional intelligence!

If you recall, we said that emotional intelligence involves using our cognitive and emotional abilities in our relationships and social groups, as well as in managing our state of emotional being and behaviour. We have also talked about tests that are used to identify which people have a higher level of emotional intelligence. Some of those well-known tests, such as the Mayer-Salovey-Caruso Emotional Intelligence Test (MSCEIT) tend to show women having a higher emotional intelligence ability than men, although this is not universally upheld by all academics in the field. For example, brain neuroimaging and other behavioural tests seem to dispute this, and yet, self-assessment tests relating to empathy indicate that women seem to possess more than men.

But that's not to say that men don't have empathy, or are not capable of acquiring it. Neither does it mean that women have some genetic predisposition that gives them a head start over men. At the end of the day, it may have more to do with the way we are raised than anything else. If you are a man, the chances are that as you were growing up, you were discouraged from crying, because boys don't do that. Boys and men who are openly emotional are often seen as effeminate in some circles. No one wants to be laughed at or made fun of, so it is natural to learn to hide such behaviour or to train ourselves to avoid it as we grow older. Being 'masculine' carries a heavily defined agenda, even today, and although recent trends encourage men to express their emotions, we aren't quite there yet.

On the other hand, no one ever told a girl not to cry, and it is viewed as something quite natural when women burst into tears. Those women who aren't overly expressive in that respect are often labelled as cold and insensitive. Is it a no-win situation? Absolutely not!

As we come to understand more about psychology, neurology and anthropology, a lot of information has come to light about the physiological differences between men and women, and also regarding their similarities and potential. A few years ago, I stumbled across a book by Steve Biddulph, a family therapist and parenting author. In his book, entitled Raising Boys, I was pleasantly surprised to learn that there are indeed differences between the two genders and Biddulph explains very well in which way boys differ from girls. First published in 1998, the groundbreaking book was an important addition to the dialogue surrounding how men have also had a bad deal, often being deprived of the opportunity to grow into fully rounded human beings. Not only that, he goes on to explain how it is possible to help boys to be happy, well-balanced men.

If you can relate to this, then I hope that you can find something in this book that will empower you, whether you are a father, mother, brother, sister, partner or friend.

Piles and piles of studies have been carried out on emotional intelligence and the differences between how men and women in this area. I can't begin to discuss all of them in this book, and I also don't wish to bore you. Suffice to say that there are many factors to consider when investigating the subject, such as age, ethnicity, socioeconomic and educational levels, as well as where you were raised.

Traditionally, it's women who have been seen as experiencing positive and negative emotions more intensely than men, which is a stereotype that we are all familiar with. Basically, women are seen as more emotional than men, with evidence from biochemistry being used to support this claim. The argument goes that women are better prepared for survival, with certain parts of their brain dedicated to emotional processing being larger than those in men's brains. We also have the social argument, which claims that women receive an education biased towards the emotional, which men are taught to minimize. Does that apply to you?

How do you respond when you see some tragic news playing out somewhere in the world on your TV screen? Does it come easy to you to let your emotions take over, or do you swallow them? Doing either one or the other isn't wrong – but learning to recognize your emotions is a big step.

Realising that you do feel compassion, empathy and sorrow will lead you to experience a fuller life in which you are more in touch with your emotions and better able to manage them, instead of ignoring them.

What is the first thing that a baby does when it is born? It cries. If it doesn't, then that's a problem which will send the whole maternity team spinning into action. Although the instinct of the newborn to cry is a way to clear the lungs of fluid, it is also the very first expression we make in this world – a cry, a scream, a yell – that's the sign of a healthy child!

As recruiters begin to realise that women are better than men in dealing with interpersonal relationships through their use of a positive tone, and empathizing with others, the onus is on men to get their act together. There is also a theory that men and women's brains are just made differently, with the feminine brain more designed for empathy while the male brain is designed to understand and construct systems. It's food for thought, but if that is the case, how come many men are very emotionally intelligent, while many women are not?

On the whole, the size of gender differences in emotional intelligence is said to be very small and although women seem to have the upper hand in most of the studies coming out, that is not to say that men cannot be more emotionally intelligent. What we need to remember is that once we start talking about gender as an explanatory factor of behavior, we are always operating within a very complex environment of things like demographics and socio-cultural norms.

Think of someone you know who is a leader – it could be the coach of your local soccer team or your President. What qualities do they need to fulfill their position? Strength, determination, integrity, or anything else? Ask yourself now if they should also have and express empathy. Your answer will determine how you see emotional intelligence. If you answered yes, then no matter if that leader is a male or female, they need to learn how to be empathetic. If your answer was no, then maybe it's time to redefine your perception of what a leader should be.

Women are taking up more and more leadership roles in businesses as employers begin to appreciate the value of a wider range of qualities to successfully lead teams and companies. It's never too late to learn new skills, and even learning one aspect of emotional intelligence such as better communication can help you to pursue your dreams with greater ease, no matter what gender you are.

PART TWO

DEVELOP YOUR MENTAL STRENGTH

<u>Manage your life with emotional intelligence</u>

Life is full of ups and downs, and our emotions too.

We can go through a wide range of emotions on any single day, from excitement to stress or enthusiasm to disappointment. It's not something that we consciously seem to think about – we just feel the way we do at any given moment. These emotions are triggered by events that we don't pay much attention to, sometimes becoming habits or a way of life.

For example, if you have a long commute every day, you may often feel mentally exhausted by the time you reach the workplace. It starts the moment you open your eyes in the morning:

- It's 6.30 am
- The alarm goes off (that in itself is a form of torture)
- You jump out of bed (stress levels begin to rise)
- Have a shower, get dressed (what to wear?)
- Grab a coffee or a slice of toast (not the best way to enjoy breakfast)
- Jump in the car or run to the bus stop (it's you against the clock now)
- Stuck in morning rush hour traffic (stress levels increasing)
- You miss the bus/train/metro (stress levels at the max)
- You get to work late (your boss is not happy)

By the time you take up your work post or sit at your desk, you may feel like you have already run the gauntlet and could be agitated, upset, frustrated or angry. Those feelings can follow you around all day. You are snappy with your colleagues, rude to clients, sulking whenever you see your boss and defensive when asked to do something. Does this sound familiar?

I used to live in a wonderful rural cottage surrounded by country fields and woods. It was an extremely peaceful setting just 60 miles away from the city centre, where I worked. Each day, I would make the commute to the office by car on the highway, with traffic making what should be a 20-minute journey more of a 50-minute saga. Finding a parking spot was also always a problem on arrival in town, with the county parking lot operating on a first-come, first-served basis. Sometimes it would take me 15 minutes to find a spot.

As manager of an administration team, the feeling of arriving late after everyone else did not set a good example, and that thought raised my stress levels from the moment I left home. By the time I managed to sit at my desk, I was already feeling completely exhausted. This was reflected in my work, my relationships with my colleagues and my sense of self-worth. The solution wasn't to wake up earlier, which seemed impossible for me to do, or to move nearer to my work, as I truly loved my home. I felt miserable and was almost ready to quit.

Often, we find ourselves immersed in daily routines and situations which take their toll on our emotional wellbeing. The example above is a common one, and you can probably think of many more. What is important to remember is this: we may not be able to change our circumstances, but we can change the way we deal with the emotions that they produce.

My first piece of advice would be to avoid letting emotions spiral out of control in the first place, by taking preventative measures. But of course, there will often be times when events cannot be anticipated or planned for. That is where emotional intelligence comes in, as we learn how to master our emotions, rather than vice versa.

Managing your life with emotional intelligence doesn't mean not having emotions, or negating your feelings. Quite the opposite – it means being conscious of your emotions and managing them in a way that is not detrimental to your wellbeing. Some call it mindfulness or being emotionally present, in which you are aware of how you feel but can master those impulses before they override your thoughts and self-control.

We'll talk a lot in Section 3 about practical ways in which to handle emotions so just bear in mind for the moment that help is on the way. Sometimes, we don't realize that there is a problem until we suffer a health issue or face confrontation from friends or peers. It's difficult to see how our behaviour is affecting others when we are running on blindly. You may get used to being in a constant state of stress or anxiety, but there will be repercussions sooner or later.

By not taking control of your emotions, you are creating more chances of failure, lack of success in your relationships and career, and exposing yourself to possible health risks. On top of all that, you just won't enjoy life to the full.

Begin by simply taking the time to notice your emotional responses and consider what may be behind them. How do your values play a part in that, or your memories and experiences?

When I thought about quitting my job, I couldn't see the woods for the trees and was at rock-bottom. It was time to make some changes and I didn't know where to start so I decided to talk to my line manager about the stress I was under.

To my surprise, she said that she hadn't noticed me being late, and was reasonably happy with my work output. It struck me that, in many ways, my obsession with punctuality was something that I had enforced on myself. I remembered getting a black mark on the school register for not being on time when I was in second grade, which I had felt very ashamed of – punctuality was a big thing at my school then.

That feeling of shame had stayed with me for so many years, causing me to suffer high levels of stress if I felt that I wasn't going to be somewhere on time. Once I detected where that feeling was coming from (thanks to my memory), I began to work on putting it in its rightful place and within context. I slowly began to enjoy my morning drive to work and focussed less on the time and more on the scenery.

As always, the emotions that we experience are self-generated, mismanaged and if left to their own devices, can transform into ogres. It's time to stop that from happening.

Better communication for better results

It's one thing to know how you feel, and quite another to communicate that effectively.

Getting a grip on your emotions takes practise and once you are able to do that, you can also learn to understand others better. This opens up the lines of communication in your relationships, your workplace and even with complete strangers.

Have you ever noticed how it is even easier to talk to a stranger than with a friend or colleague? Why is that? Could it be because you don't feel that a stranger will judge you, or make any preconceived assumptions about you? Maybe it is also because they have a neutral standpoint, not knowing you personally, and will not step over the line and push any of your buttons.

You may have even undergone therapy of some kind in the past with a professional psychologist or counsellor and found it relatively easy to talk about exactly how you feel.

That's all well and good. But being able to communicate effectively on an everyday basis with your nearest and dearest is key if you desire richer, more fruitful relationships. And communication isn't just about talking - it's also about being a good listener!

Better communication means less conflict, more collaboration and better results for everyone. A person with a high EQ is more able to manage conflicts when they arise and to build meaningful relationships, They can grasp the issue at hand easier than someone with a lesser level of EQ and therefore address what needs to be done more successfully. This ability has a positive impact on those involved and it has been proven that good leaders have a relatively high EQ. Those who lead badly act defensively, escalate conflict and do not succeed at resolving problems, nor do they gain the support of their team.

Imagine a basketball coach screaming at his players during a crucial game and throwing tantrums at the referee's decisions. That game isn't going to end well. His team will be despondent, frustrated, disappointed and unable to function successfully. You may have a superior who reacts the same way that, instead of encouraging the employees, is constantly picking on their faults and weaknesses. It could be that your partner is passive-aggressive and instead of speaking their mind, acts begrudgingly or goes off into a sulk. This is not the way to communicate.

The raging basketball coach or the bad-tempered partner have a problem – they don't know how to deal with their emotions. When you are aware of your own emotions or those of others, you are more likely to succeed in communicating with people. Just as the way that you feel affects others, noticing how other people feel will affect your approach to them. Making someone understand you is paramount and listening to another person helps to establish stronger bonds and better working relationships. And don't forget – we communicate with more than just words - our whole body language gives away a lot of cues, as well as the things that we DON'T say.

If you want to be a better communicator, begin with a simple experiment:

Sit in front of a mirror and pretend that you are talking to a colleague who you are upset with. How will you begin the dialogue? Will it be a full-frontal criticism and moan, or an explanation of how you really feel?

Now try imagining that you are listening to their response. Look in the mirror and check your facial expression – are you conveying the right emotions? Is it clear how you feel? How do you think your colleague will react?

Here are 5 practical skills to aid you in communicating better:

1. Consider other people's feelings.
Listen with intention to what others have to say and focus on how their words describe their feelings. Consider what else is going on in their life to explain their reaction when they talk to you. Often, it is not about anything we have done, but how that person is feeling about their own life.

2. Consider your own feelings.
Your feelings can get in the way of your communication too. Having a stressful morning can affect the way you react to others. Pay attention to that and don't let it interfere with the message you want to get across. Even if you are feeling ecstatic or enthusiastic, it can interfere with the lines of communication, so be conscious of that.

3. Have empathy.
Empathy is one of the most important traits that anyone can have, as it enables you to understand and relate to how others are feeling. Once you're able to put yourself in their shoes, you can recognize another person's feelings and comprehend them better. Empathy also nurtures trust and mutual understanding, which is essential to any relationship.

4. Create trust.

Building trust between yourself and the person with whom you're communicating is very important. Listening intently, maintaining eye contact and giving non-verbal cues that you understand lets them know that you hear and relate to them.

5. Spot misunderstandings.

Emotional awareness can help you to avoid misunderstandings, which are often the result of confusing emotions or signals. Recognize that a friend may be upset about something and approach you in an angry manner. Don't take it personally – it isn't about you, so avoid becoming a part of their problem by retaliating aggressively.

Often, we need to step back from a situation and think about what we are feeling before we engage in a dialogue that could accelerate conflict. After all, why burn bridges when you can build them instead? Learning how to empower yourself through emotional intelligence will help you avoid conflict and create more coherent, honest relationships with people in your circle, as well as with yourself.

What is self-awareness?

Imagine that you are a 100-meter sprinter.

Your every step is perfectly calculated, from head to toe. Each movement is a sequence of highly-trained techniques designed to make you the fastest. The muscles in your body are in total unison, working to their limits as you aim for the finish line. It takes physical strength, discipline, stamina, concentration and years of training to be good at it. Your mind and body are finely-tuned to one purpose alone; to win.

Now imagine that we are talking about being self-aware.

How much attention do you ever pay to that? What amount of time and effort have you put into really knowing yourself? Are you as familiar with yourself as a sprinter is with his or her body?

Those are tough questions, aren't they? You may have never even thought about the subject before, or feel that it isn't relevant to you. Most of us go through each day on a kind of autopilot, without thinking too much about anything more than what we need to do, plans for tomorrow, how to get through the week, and so on. All of our habits, routines, reactions and decisions seem to manifest themselves without us having to think about them at all. We just don't spend that much time on self-knowledge – we know who we are, right?

The important thing to remember about being on autopilot is this: you aren't in control.

Going through the motions doesn't mean that you know why you respond the way that you do in any given situation. You aren't really conscious of that. Most of us don't stop to think every time we feel happy, sad, upset, angry, blissful or frustrated. But by having better self-awareness, you can change the way you experience life, bringing you more clarity about how you handle challenges and enabling you to overcome hurdles and achieve your goals. It can also give you a much better understanding of how others affect you.

For example, imagine that your best friend calls you up to cry on your shoulder about a recent break-up with a partner, and you end up feeling equally down after the call has ended. It spoils the rest of my day as you carry that negative feeling around with you, maybe even bringing up memories of failed relationships in your own past. Being more self-aware of your feelings will equip you with the tools to avoid absorbing someone else's negative experiences and protect you from the knock-on effect of that.

Sound good? I bet you are wondering what the secret is. Well, self-awareness is simply knowing yourself better. Once you reach that level of understanding, you are much more in control of every aspect of your life, from emotions to actions. It's that simple.

A standard definition of 'self-awareness' is the ability to see yourself clearly through reflection and introspection. It's about monitoring your feelings and emotions, which are triggered so often by things that you are hardly conscious of. It is not about self-blame or self-criticism, so bear that in mind as we go through this chapter and don't be too hard on yourself. Here, we are talking about being honest with yourself, without judgement.

Practising self-awareness has four main benefits:

- It can make you more proactive, boost your acceptance, and encourage positive self-development.
- It can allow you to see things from the perspective of others, practice better self-control, work more creatively and experience pride in your work and accomplishments.
- It can give you better decision-making skills.
- It can make you perform better at work, develop better communication

with people and enhance your self-confidence.

Of course, the benefits are not exhaustive by any means, and by tapping into your unconscious reactions and emotions, you can begin to enhance virtually every aspect of your life. It isn't a miracle cure – it takes work and dedication – but if you are up for it, the journey will definitely be worthwhile. By learning to evaluate yourself in every situation, you will be able to make better choices and enrich your daily life, and who wouldn't want that! So, how aware of yourself, your inner self, are you?

Let's take a small test to find out.

I am going to make some simple statements. For each one, think about whether you strongly disagree, disagree somewhat, agree, agree somewhat or strongly agree. There are no right or wrong answers here, so just go with what your gut instinct tells you, without thinking about your responses too much.

1. I know how to maintain my happiness.
2. I believe that I can learn how to increase my happiness.
3. I have a good work-life balance.
4. I rarely feel stressed.
5. I feel good about myself.
6. I think positively.
7. I can calm myself down after an upsetting experience.
8. I stay present in every moment.
9. I know what matters most to me.
10. I have meaningful relationships with others.
11. I eat foods that nourish both my mind and body.
12. I am happy.
13. I am ready to make the effort to increase my happiness.

Which statements did you strongly agree with, and which ones not so much? Whatever your answers are, that is fine. This test isn't a critique of your personality or character. It is simply an opportunity to reflect on how you feel about some aspects of your life. You may, for instance, strongly disagree with statement 6, which states that you think positively. If you do disagree, now is a good time to ask yourself what is stopping you from being more positive. Is it because of let-downs in the past, or is it more to do with not feeling confident in yourself at this moment? Are you feeling insecure about the future?

It's quite possible that you won't be able to explain right away why you don't feel positive. And that is OK too. Self-awareness can't be bought over the counter like fast food – it needs time and patience before you can begin to enjoy it. Think of it as a slow-cooked casserole – well worth the wait!

If you strongly agree with all of the above statements, then that is great. You are on the right track. If you agree with some points, and not others, spend some time looking more deeply at the statements which you disagree with and consider how they impact aspects of your life on a daily basis. If, for example, you disagree somewhat with statement 7, I can calm myself down after an upsetting experience, try to recall the last time that you felt like this. What happened? How did it affect you? Could you have avoided it?

Once again, I am not suggesting that you kick yourself for acting in one way or another. Self-awareness is simply about observing yourself in a particular situation and seeing how you respond to it. Monitoring how you feel and react will provide you with valuable insights about how to manage your emotions in the future. Forget about 'why' you felt the way you did, and instead, concentrate on 'how' it made you feel. This is the key to understanding yourself more.

Be a fly on the wall

Observe your responses and reactions as if you were a fly on the wall.

When you stand back and become an impartial observer, you can get a much better idea of the whole picture. The next time you feel stressed, which can be debilitating, examine how you are feeling. Are you in panic mode? Do you feel unable to concentrate?? Are you afraid that something will go badly? Instead of simply experiencing these things, turn your attention inwards to your emotions and look at them as if they belonged to someone else. What is triggering them? How can they be better managed? What advice would you give to yourself?

This is an exercise in achieving self-awareness and emotional intelligence that you can do any time, any place.

Setting the standards

There's nothing more stressful than going for a job interview. It's a common example of a situation where you may feel that you are being personally evaluated and assessed. How many interviews have you come out of feeling that things didn't go well? What about when you were rejected for a position? How useless did it make you feel? Yes, I get you – it has happened to almost all of us at least once. That sense of being 'not good enough' can stay with you for a long time, and you probably blame yourself for not being successful. All legitimate reactions, right?

In actual fact, therapist's offices are full of people who feel that they can't achieve their high standards – standards which they have personally imposed on themselves. This will never lead to success, because if the bar that we set is too high for us, how can we ever reach it? Part of self-awareness is realizing that, and shifting the bar to a level which is more attainable. Not getting that job may be due to an infinite number of reasons that have nothing to do with your performance. You may simply have not been what the company was looking for.

When you engage in self-evaluation, you can give some thought to whether you are thinking, feeling and acting as you "should" or behaving according to norms. Most likely, you compare your behaviour in line with your own standards of correctness, through which you judge yourself and others. Often, we set ourselves up for failure, believing that we are unable to change how we react to a given situation, which prevents us from trying to correct it.

There is nothing worse than feeling that you don't match up to your standards. This creates a feeling of failure, self-loathing, and self-hate. It seems to be easier to avoid trying to fix this altogether, but that is a mistake. Instead of self-induced negativity, which will become a pattern that affects all of your future actions, be an impartial observer. Look at how you behave or feel and focus on realigning yourself with your true capabilities and potential. By the same token, apply this to those around you – be their fly on the wall and you will achieve a greater understanding of their behaviour towards you.

This begins by being honest with yourself.

What is anxiety, and do you suffer from it?

We are all programmed to suffer from anxiety.

It's a natural reaction to stress and everyone experiences it. Whether it's your wedding day or you are about to make a public speech, feelings of insecurity and nervousness are bound to rise up. Your brain kicks into action to deal with what it sees as a threat or danger by releasing stress hormones like adrenaline and cortisol. Once the 'threatening' situation is over, your body will usually return to normal again.

Whenever we feel anxious like that, there is usually a good reason: after all, it's not every day that you get married and, even if you are used to public speaking, a little bit of stage fright is completely normal. Your reactions subside once the moment has passed and you can literally 'breathe a sigh of relief'.

Taking an important exam is a good example. No matter how much you have studied for it, the fear of failure, self-doubt and insecurity can turn you into a nervous wreck before you even enter the exam room. But once you sit down and start writing, your brain reboots and gets down to working for you in the way that it should. Your logic kicks in and all of those 'fight or flight' hormones seem to magically disappear.

When bouts of anxiety last for longer periods of time for no apparent reason, then that may become an actual disorder, which can strongly impair the quality of your life and those around you. Studies show that many people suffer from extreme anxiety, with approximately 1 in 4 having some sort of long-term anxiety during their lifespan; that's a lot of people. The good news is that those who are identified as having a higher level of emotional intelligence suffer much less from deep-rooted anxiety, and can deal with stressful situations much more effectively than those who don't. So there is light at the end of the tunnel if you are one of those 1 in 4.

Learning the right coping mechanisms for anxiety can improve your quality of life and help you to function more effectively, no matter what is thrown at you. But how do you know if you suffer from anxiety, and what are the symptoms?

I want you to think very carefully about the following statements and just answer YES or NO to each one:

- Do you worry about a lot of things?
- Do you think you worry excessively?
- Do you worry more days than not?
- Have you been worrying like this for the past 6 months?
- Is it hard for you to control your worrying?
- Do you have any physical symptoms such as restlessness, feeling tired, trouble concentrating, irritability, muscle tension, or sleep issues?
- Does your worrying negatively impact your ability to function at school, work, or with friends and family?

If you answered YES to one or more of the questions, it is quite possible that you have what is known as an anxiety disorder. But don't panic! About 20% of the population are in the same boat as you, so that's the first thing to recognize. Secondly, there are ways to deal with anxiety so that you can return to a life free from those overwhelming feelings – just bear with me on this. By learning how to use emotional intelligence, you can help yourself to handle your thought processes, which are responsible for creating so much turmoil, and return to a state of inner balance.

You may not even be aware that you are suffering from anxiety, although your body will be trying to warn you about it. It gives you several clues, not always all at the same time, so why not sit back and think about how you may have been feeling recently and try to connect that with an incident or experience that you have recently gone through.

You may have had an increased heart rate or sense that you are breathing too fast. Possibly you have felt restless, sweaty or dizzy. And what about being unable to sleep or having nightmares? These are just some of the physical effects of anxiety, which can wreak havoc on your everyday functioning and wellbeing.

More severe forms of anxiety can include panic attacks, phobias, obsessive-compulsive disorders, separation anxiety, post-traumatic stress disorder and depression. You could even suffer from feelings of shame, isolation, anger or irritability. If you relate to any of these, then it is a good idea to seek medical help from professionals who are specialists in these areas.

Having a high EQ doesn't mean that you won't occasionally feel anxious or worry, but what it does bring to the table is more awareness of these feelings, so that they can be managed before they become a runaway train. The more in tune you are with uncomfortable emotions, the easier it is to deal with them. It's not about negating how you feel, but more about learning how to master your internal response mechanism so that you don't carry around with you all of that angst.

When my friend John left home, he found it very difficult to adapt. Although moving to a new town to start an exciting new job, he wasn't looking forward to the idea of living on his own for the first time. For the first few months, he found it almost impossible to sleep at night. He was worried about burglars breaking in and woke up at the slightest noise. Not only that: he felt lonely and insecure. His anxiety levels were so high that he avoided going home for as long as he could, preferring to work extra hours in the new company. Tiredness and lack of sleep were taking their toll on him, as well as an increasing sense of loneliness and estrangement.

What advice would you have given to John?

What would you have said to him to help him overcome his anxiety?

It's a tough situation, isn't it? I am sure that you can relate to it and have possibly experienced something very similar at some point in the past. Maybe the circumstances were different, but you can still identify with that feeling of overwhelming anxiety, which disrupts your wellbeing.

Remember what we said earlier on in this book about emotional intelligence? It involves self-awareness, self-management, empathy, social skills and motivation. Luckily, John was able to adapt those skills to improve his situation and begin to enjoy this new phase in his life. How did he do it?

- By acknowledging his anxiety, John took the first step to dealing with it. He thought about all of the reasons why being alone made him feel so vulnerable and confronted his fears head-on.
- On accepting that his reaction may be unfounded, John worked hard to boost his confidence and self-esteem, telling himself that he was fully capable of living alone.
- Next, he took positive steps to counter the negative impact of his feelings by installing more secure door locks. Whenever he went to bed, he chose to read a book to take his mind off his fears, instead of self-obsessing.
- He explained his concerns to his boss and colleagues, which alleviated him from the burden and also helped them to connect with him better and understand his predicament.
- John adopted a dog from a local shelter and now has 'someone' waiting for him to come home at night!

The most important step that John took was to recognize his anxiety and to work through it. He took control of his life again.

Often, the anxiety that we face has more to do with the way we feel when with other people and how we handle our relationships. This is known as social anxiety disorder and can keep us feeling isolated and disconnected if we are unable to deal with it.

It all comes down to fear of being judged by others in social situations.

Social anxiety explained

Are you introspective or what someone would call 'the quiet type'? Maybe you simply prefer your own company. That is absolutely fine. For many of us though, shyness makes it difficult to interact with others or can make socialising a rather unpleasant experience. It is something that we have to deal with throughout our lives and is a short-term reaction that manifests itself under certain circumstances. Being called out for a mistake you made at work can be embarrassing, and you may blush on receiving a compliment

– these are all common indicators of shyness.

Long-term shyness is something different, which can become a hurdle if you want to have a more enriching social life, or need to be more outgoing because of your work. It can develop into social anxiety (SAD) or social phobia as it is often called, which can cause real fear in social settings and totally disrupt your life.

If you suffer from this, you will know what terror can strike just on meeting new people at a social gathering. The fear is based on the idea that you will be judged or scrutinized by others. You may even begin to sense a bit of anxiety just now while reading this because the very thought of having to deal with the above situations increases your stress levels. This can all build up inside you until you avoid any form of social contact, which is very damaging in the long run.

The downside to social anxiety is that it is much more ingrained in our psyche than other behaviours and recent research has shown that it is often deeply rooted in specific past childhood experiences, unusual brain functioning or perhaps related to genetic causes. On the upside, it is an issue which can be addressed with the right help, and acknowledging your anxiety is the first step to overcoming it.

Many celebrities have openly talked about how they have suffered from social anxiety, and include names like Oprah Winfrey, Taylor Swift, Adele and actor Stephen Colbert. Most people undergo similar symptoms, such as the ones below:

• Intense fear of social interactions
• Anticipatory anxiety that leads to avoiding opportunities for conversation or public speaking
• Extreme symptoms of anxiety during unwanted or stressful social interactions
• Poor verbal communication skills
• Overly critical self-evaluations of performance
• Low self-esteem and a lack of self-confidence
• Deep-seated fears of being judged, rejected, embarrassed or humiliated
• Feelings of nausea
• Adopting a rigid body posture or making little eye contact
• Being very self-conscious in front of other people

What is going on with your brain when in a state of extreme social anxiety? If you have a brain scan there and then, it will show hyperactivity in the amygdala, which is responsible for that old 'flight or fight' response that we are becoming so accustomed to reading about. It's your internal fire alarm telling your body to respond to a perceived threat, real or imagined.

Before you know it, you are experiencing a rapid heartbeat, sweaty palms, muscle tightening, a sharp rise in blood sugar levels and brain freeze. The control tower of the brain, the prefrontal cortex, amplifies the activity instead of doing the opposite, just in the same way that a broken stoplight will cause traffic chaos. But guess what? You can recondition your brain to stop overreacting to every single response associated with anxiety, although it needs time.

It has been claimed that even those with a high EQ can suffer from social anxiety because they are more sensitive to the reactions of others and so may read more into them. At the end of the day, what matters most is not so much where you stand on the EQ scale, but how balanced you feel within yourself. I will leave you with 5 tips to help you do this, and of course, you will find more practical examples in Part Three of this book:

- Try to recognize anxiety in yourself and in others
- Begin to understand what causes your anxiety
- Learn to identify your anxiety accurately
- Attempt to express your anxiety appropriately
- Continue to regulate your anxiety effectively

As Oprah Winfrey said, *"Once you start to make changes, no matter how small, suddenly everything seems possible."*

What is low self-esteem and is it holding you back?

How much do you like yourself, on a scale of 1 to 10?

If you give yourself anything from around 5 to 8, then you are probably satisfied with most aspects of yourself and have the confidence to pursue your goals without comparing yourself to others. Anything over 8 and you may have a rather inflated idea of your capabilities, which can be a negative trait in itself, making you come off as arrogant and hostile. If you select 5 or less, then self-esteem is not your strong point and you are unlikely to have faith in yourself or your capabilities.

Self-esteem begins and ends with you – it isn't about anyone or anything else.

We all have bad days, but picking ourselves up and carrying on is usually the sign of someone with a reasonable amount of inner balance. Those who have a good level of emotional intelligence are able to look at what went wrong, adjust their behaviour or feelings accordingly, and pick up from where they left off without castigating themselves too much.

On the other hand, there are those who are unable to shake off the disapproval or criticism of family, friends, teachers or colleagues which, over time, leave them scoring very low in the self-esteem scale. It's easy to understand how that could happen, right?

It seems that self-esteem fluctuates as we grow older, rising and falling depending on our experiences, but it steadies itself around the age of 60 until old age sets in. That's a long time to wait if you are still in your twenties, thirties or forties and suffering from more lows than highs. Having little self-esteem can impact your life enormously, from your academic and professional success to your relationships, mental health and overall view of life.

What is so important about self-esteem in relation to emotional intelligence? Well, no one wants to feel inferior to others. We all want to fit in, be able to lead a full life and achieve our goals. If you tell yourself that you have no worth or value, then life is always going to be an uphill struggle for you, because obviously, you just don't 'have what it takes'. To get to the top of the mountain, you have to take the first step and if you refuse to do so because you don't think you are capable, you will remain at the bottom forever. Wouldn't you like to enjoy the views from the top?

Life brings us many challenges every day and if we all felt that we were unable to cope, we might as well pull down the shutters, draw the curtains and stay in bed. This isn't to say that if you have low self-esteem you are a loser – it simply means that you haven't yet found a way to overcome your negativity.

There may be times when you fail at something, make a mistake, or mess up. These are all completely normal occurrences that everyone experiences often. If you have a healthy level of self-esteem, you will handle these hiccups and judge their importance, learning and growing from them. But if you have little self-esteem, each small knock, error or trip-up will bring you further and further down. Getting out of that negative cycle can be difficult, especially if you had very little confidence in yourself to begin with.

The first step on that path is to recognize that you are suffering from low self-esteem, which you may not have even focused on. You may have been so busy wallowing in 'I am useless' thoughts that you didn't give yourself the opportunity to step out of the box and examine your emotions and behavior. Now is a good time to do that.

Here are some examples of self-esteem issues. I want you to think about which ones you strongly relate to or feel describe you.

1. You like to please people
2. You are easily angered or irritated
3. You feel that your opinion isn't important
4. Nothing that you do is ever good enough
5. You're highly sensitive to others opinions
6. You feel that the world is unsafe
7. You often feel sad and worthless
8. You find it hard to maintain relationships
9. You avoid taking risks or trying out new things
10. You find it difficult to set boundaries with others
11. You pay more attention to your weaknesses
12. You often feel unsure of who you are
13. You struggle to say no
14. You find it difficult to ask for help or support
15. You have a pessimistic outlook on life
16. You doubt your chances of success
17. You frequently experience negative emotions, such as fear, anxiety or depression
18. You often compare yourself with others and come in second best

If you can identify with several of these points, then you are probably lacking in self-esteem. Each one of them can be truly damaging to your sense of wellbeing, so it is important to be honest with yourself and concentrate on the points that ring a bell with you. Feeling pessimistic about your capabilities, your ability to have fulfilling relationships and your chances of future success can prevent you from even trying to achieve anything worthwhile in life. The serious side to this is mental illness, poor health, social isolation and depression.

There is an abundance of research related to low self-esteem and the results speak for themselves. Looking at adolescents, we have learnt that low self-esteem is associated with violence, school drop-out rates, teenage pregnancy, suicide and low academic achievement – not surprising if you think about it, right?

Teenagers with low self-esteem are more likely to relate their sense of worth to their weight and body shape and around 7 out of 10 don't feel that they're 'good enough'. Even girls as young as 10 are in fear of being fat and many teenagers have eating disorders or want to change a part of their physical appearance. That's a very sad reflection on the world we live in, and those teenagers will one day grow up to be fully-fledged adults. If they continue to have such negative opinions of themselves, how will they ever be able to achieve their life goals?

How low self-esteem develops

Where is all of this negativity coming from? Why are you so down on yourself? If you can get to the bottom of that, then you will be able to untangle those knots and begin to restore your sense of self-worth.

There are several factors which seem to influence our self-esteem, including genetics, personality, age and health. In addition, things like our social circumstances, thoughts and the reaction of others can have a negative impact. Having said that, low self-esteem is something that can be improved on once it is identified. You may suffer from temporary bouts of low self-esteem due to some setback, or go through a period in which things are just not going your way. Establishing a strong central core, or sense of self-worth is the key to helping you bounce back.

Can you think of an instance when you felt that you had hit rock-bottom? How did you respond to the situation? How did you get back to normal? Did that feeling of uselessness last for a long period of time, even well after the event?

Although low self-esteem is an internal view of ourselves, that view can be formed and reinforced by external events, people and situations. It can be a number of factors and although in isolation, they may not seem so bad, if one or more occur, they could really influence the way we feel about ourselves.

Often, when couples separate or go through a divorce, that can have a tremendous effect on one's self of worth. If you have experienced a break-up, you may have internalised it to the point where you felt that you did something wrong, or were not good enough. This is a very common reaction when betrayal is involved, as you compare yourself to the 'new' partner. Instead of believing in your value as a person, you actually devalue yourself in the face of competition. Those involved in long-term, happy relationships with a spouse or partner don't usually feel that way, and have no issues with self-esteem.

The same applies if you have a good job, where you feel respected and valued. Because work identity is positively related to self-esteem. If you are fired, you may slump into a feeling of dejection for a while, until the next job offer comes along. I remember being unemployed for a good few months after graduation and can still recall that feeling of worthlessness. It didn't help that all of my fellow graduates had found jobs almost immediately, and I was beginning to wonder what was 'wrong' with me. That's not a good place to be!

Coming from an underprivileged background has proven to be a large factor in increasing low self-esteem, where opportunities for advancement may seem few and far between. Think of a young person who cannot afford to enter into further education and is trapped in a cycle of poverty and you will get the picture.

Living alone has also been linked with low self-esteem, whenever that is an enforced situation and not a life choice. Many people are quite happy living a solitary life without a better half, but for others, it can increase feelings of insecurity, loneliness and despair. Those who are housebound or have some sort of mobility disability may also go through periods of feeling very low, although that does not mean that it is the case for everyone. It is probably linked to other factors too.

Social pressures can play a large part in your self-esteem, which brings me to the subject of social media. If you are spending large portions of your time scrolling through your Instagram or Facebook feed, this can have a detrimental effect on you, as you are bombarded with images of people who seem slimmer, happier, more beautiful, cleverer, more successful, etc. Hands up if you are guilty of this!

While most of us have fully incorporated both the good and the bad aspects of social media into our lives, the downside is that we use those around us as a measure of ourselves. Have you ever wished that you were as beautiful as Kim Kardashian (or as rich) or were having a fantastic time jumping off waterfalls in some exotic location for a living? Actually, don't you sometimes feel so envious of those gorgeous 'influencers' and their 'fabulous' lifestyles?

Although we know that this isn't real life, we choose to believe that it is, as we compare our own boring existence with those perfect faces, bodies and achievements. If you don't feel particularly good about yourself, you are adding fuel to the fire when you buy into the false realities of social media. Even commenting on a topical feed and receiving a backlash of comments from 'trolls' who disagree with you can be very disheartening and get under your skin. It is like a form of self-punishment.

If you are pretty well-balanced, have a reasonable amount of self-esteem and are in tune with your emotions, you will take anything you see on social media with a large dose of salt. If you have some underlying insecurities about your own persona, it can be a harsh environment and not conducive to making you feel better about yourself. Moderation is the key here, and filling your social media feed with inspirational content, rather than carefully fabricated ideals of perfection. After all, no one is perfect!

How your attitude affects your mental state

Our brain tells us whatever it wants and usually, we listen to it. It's our best tool for getting through life. By the same token, it can be our worst enemy. When it (your brain or inner voice) keeps telling you that you are not as good as everyone else, after a while, you begin to believe it. We actually brainwash ourselves!

And with that constant reminder that we are not 'good enough', 'brave enough', 'smart enough', beautiful enough', it's very easy how we will slowly lose our sense of self-esteem over time. On the other hand, if you tell yourself that you are smart, funny, able, good company, confident, this will make you feel more content.

Imagine that you recently took your driving test for the first time, and failed. If you have a good level of self-esteem, you will acknowledge your mistakes, such as not studying enough, or admit you didn't do the reverse parking so well, or you simply had an off day. You don't start ranting to yourself about how you are stupid and will probably fail the test again when you next take it. Instead, you have a healthy sense of reality, can think critically about why you failed and try harder next time. You also won't equate that failure with lack of success in general in your life and wallow in self-pity. Sure, you may feel bad, but you bounce back pretty easily, and it doesn't prevent you from having a laugh over it with your friends or going about your normal business with a smile.

Our self-esteem plays a significant role in how we see the rest of the world. It shapes our perception of ourselves and others. When you suffer from a lack of self-esteem, you are giving yourself a 1 out of 10, instead of a 6,7 or 8. Other people are the 8s, right? Putting yourself down isn't good for you, and it can affect all aspects of your life, from your job to your relationships.

We will look in Part Three at critical ways of regaining self-esteem, but for now, let's ponder on how low self-esteem can colour your whole world and have dire long-term effects.

If you recognize any of these traits in yourself, I want you to hold that thought and consider how much it is affecting your happiness and wellbeing:

1. Inability to handle stress
2. Have some kind of eating disorder
3. Feel worthless, guilty or ashamed
4. Unable to be assertive and express yourself
5. Find it hard to build strong, lasting relationships
6. May be in a toxic relationship
7. Find it difficult to make good decisions
8. Easily put off by setbacks, failures and disappointments
9. Indulge in unhealthy habits, such as smoking or drinking
10. Feel pessimistic about the future

Make no doubt about it – this is not a good place to be. All of the above can have a negative impact on your life, health and happiness if left to fester and grow. You may think that some of them are no big deal, such as being unable to assert or express yourself. That is the same as asking people to treat you like a doormat, which they will if given the chance. Once you begin to stand up for yourself and voice your opinion in an assertive manner, you are establishing your boundaries and your value. This can bring you more success at work, be able to resolve conflicts easier with family and friends, as well as improving your overall view on life.

Self-esteem is not a quick-fix for all of your problems, but it will arm you with the tools to try new things, face challenges, build up resilience to set-backs and help you to look forward instead of back. It is a long-term project, which you can achieve with hard work and a belief in yourself.

Why procrastination is holding you back

How long does it take you to get around to doing something?

Putting things off doesn't seem like such a bad thing. That project you have to finish by 5 pm today will get done. You just need to do something mindless first like scroll through your social media feed for about half an hour. You keep saying that you are going to cut the lawn, but it can wait a few more days. It's no big deal. You will have time to get it done, but you just can't get around to starting right away.

That's procrastination and, even though it seems like no great personality flaw, it is a bad habit that could also be viewed as 'time-wasting'. I'm not one for watching the clock and having the regimented routine of the marine corps, but I have to admit that the more I delay tasks, the less time I seem to have to complete them. It makes sense, doesn't it?

The truth is that those of us who procrastinate don't do it because we are very bad at gauging how much time is available to us or because we are lazy, which has been the general view up until recently. We do it because we lack self-regulation and self-discipline. Once we recognize that, we can stop feeling guilty and look deeper into our emotional wellbeing to see what is preventing us from accomplishing the tasks that lie ahead of us. A lot of it has to do with self-compassion and emotional regulation.

When you put off doing anything, you know by experience that it inevitably leads to missed deadlines, a lower quality result, having to make excuses to others, and also to yourself. This has a damaging outcome in the long run for our overall sense of wellbeing. It's another example of how we often shoot ourselves in the foot, knowing that it is preventable, but doing it anyway. And what is worse is that, instead of doing what we are supposed to be doing, we can find a million other things that seem much more 'important'.

If you begin your day knowing that you have to do your weekly grocery run, but instead, spend half the morning watching some 'really interesting' YouTube videos, chat to your friends for an hour or so, have another coffee and then decide to read that new book, before you know it, it's lunchtime. You have 'wasted' the whole morning instead of getting on with the task in hand. Chances are, you will rush to the local store later on in the afternoon only to find that they are out of your favorite brand of yogurt and that there is such a big line at the checkout that you are beginning to get completely frazzled. You are also going to be late for your meet-up with friends now, who are always complaining that you never arrive on time. Hmm… where did the day go?

At the end of such an experience, you have probably run through the usual emotions of stress, anxiety, self-loathing and feelings of incompetency, never mind letting your friends down once again. That is not an empowering mindset to have. Quite the opposite – you will be beating yourself up, feeling frustrated and stressed out. The good news is that you can turn your procrastination around and prevent it from happening in the future by tapping into your emotional intelligence.

The first thing to remember is that procrastination is a choice. It can be defined like this:

"The voluntary, needless delay of an intended course of action past the time most likely to produce the desired performance or successful completion."

The word 'voluntary' is key here: we choose to do what we do – it's not a magnetic force of physics that pulls us away from a planned task – it's a decision that we make. We choose to do something else, for many reasons. It may be that the said task is difficult, boring, time-consuming or any other reason that we can think of. We know that we have to do it, and that sense of being obliged can make it seem even more unattractive. Let's be honest, who really enjoys cleaning the house? Certainly not me.

The problem is that we tell ourselves that it isn't a decision; we just can't help ourselves. What is really going on is much more subtle. When we put off a task or chore, often we are using procrastination as a way to make ourselves feel good. If you are upset about an argument with your partner, you aren't going to be in the mood to take the car for a wash. You want to do something that feeds your pleasure needs, like napping or watching TV. The outcome of this approach can be a sense of anxiety or even shame. You didn't do what you were supposed to do.

Procrastination can arise from a fear of failure - it's easy to engage in activities that carry no investment to our happiness rather than having to challenge ourselves or put our neck on the line. We learn to avoid the possibility of failure by not even attempting to start the task. This impacts our self-esteem, because deep down inside, we know that we should be doing something different, so we feel like a failure anyway. The more we put things off, the more we undermine ourselves and the more self-loathing we acquire.

A study in 2014 by Dr Fuschia Sirois, professor of psychology at the University of Sheffield found that when someone procrastinates, not only are they aware that they are avoiding the task in question, but they also know that it is a bad idea to do so, and yet, they do it anyway. That makes procrastination irrational because it doesn't make sense to do something that you know is going to have a negative outcome on your wellbeing. Not finishing that assignment on time because you spent 3 hours playing League of Legends is a catastrophe, and you know it.

It's basically your way of coping with challenging emotions and negative moods induced by boredom, anxiety, insecurity, frustration, resentment and self-doubt. It's not a time-management problem - it's an emotional regulation problem. In trying to deal with those negative moods, you look

for a quick-fix, which leads to putting off the task that you have to do.
When you do eventually get around to the job, you have associated so many negative emotions with it that you feel even more stressed out and anxious, as well as wallowing in even greater self-blame and low self-esteem. It is a vicious cycle that you continue to play, on repeat. By acquiring greater emotional intelligence, it is possible to break this bad habit and to take control of how you view yourself and how you feel. Then you will be in a better position to handle tasks more productively, which will boost your self-esteem rather than lower it.

Let's think about if you procrastinate by answering the following questions:

1. Do you delay making a decision until it is too late?
2. Do you delay before starting on work that you have to do?
3. Do you often find yourself running out of time?
4. Do you often delay acting on a decision, once made?
5. Do you waste a lot of time on trivial things?
6. Do you often find yourself completing tasks that you had planned to do days ago?
7. Do you continually say, "I'll do it tomorrow?"
8. Do you rarely complete things on time?
9. Are you bad at meeting deadlines?
10. Have you ever lost something of value because of putting things off until the last minute?

If you answer yes to at least one of the above, then this chapter is definitely for you. Apart from the practical implications that procrastination may bring to your life, such as being late for work or failing to make timely decisions that could cost you money, there are other serious effects related to your health. As the cycle goes on, chronic stress can set in, with symptoms of depression and anxiety, which we know can lead to hypertension, cardiovascular disease and other illnesses. Remember, we are what we think and our brain-body relationship is an undisputed fact.

So, why are you procrastinating when you know that it is bad for you? Well, that's because we are hard-wired to prioritize short-term needs rather than long-term ones, which is a throwback to when we had to do that to survive. In a way, we disassociate our present selves from our future selves, and our brain tells us that those future tasks are someone else's problem. That's our way of avoiding negative future feelings or distress. When faced with an unpleasant task, our amygdala (the threat detector) hijacks our common sense, telling us to avoid the oncoming collision.

So, what is important here is to address the reason for your procrastination and to apply the tools to overcome it. After all, procrastination is about emotions, it isn't about productivity, and the sooner you realize that, the better. Breaking the negative cycle requires more than just downloading an app that prevents you from having access to your internet for a certain amount of time. If you can't give your brain a better reward than putting something off, it isn't going to help you break that cycle. We have to find a better reward than avoidance, which only creates self-harm in the future.

- Self-forgiveness is one way to begin this. Forgive yourself for procrastinating, which will allow you to move past this negative behavior and focus on the next task without being weighed down by past actions.

- Self-kindness allows you to acknowledge your mistakes without self-criticizing. Instead of putting yourself down for procrastinating, think about why you are doing so and dwell on the reasons that come to mind.

- Another emotionally intelligent tool is that of self-compassion. By treating yourself with kindness and understanding, you will make room for more personal growth as your psychological stress decreases.

Typical emotions that you may go through during procrastination include things like worrying that you won't do well, being anxious about the size of the workload, feeling frustrated and not enjoying the work itself. Whatever the reason for your putting off, give yourself space to work through them and stop demonizing them because that only comes back to you as a negative experience.

When you feel more motivated, you also feel better about yourself. Being kinder to yourself releases you from regret and allows you to meet challenges with more self-acceptance, which is a very empowering trait to have. Instead of taking a negative stance about that future task, associate it with more positive attributes. Think about how proud you will feel when it is completed and that sense of satisfaction you will feel. Rather than indulging in self-criticism, take an understanding perspective of yourself in the event of failure and acknowledge your strengths and weaknesses. We all have them, but learning how to use them wisely is in our hands.

By adopting a non-judgemental approach to your emotions, you can remove yourself from the cycle of delaying in the future. By all means, get upset about procrastinating, but don't dwell on it forever. See it for what it is and instead of fixating on it, move on with greater self-awareness to your next task.

Becoming a better leader

Are you a great leader?

If your answer is yes, what qualities do you possess that make you say so? Are you tough, disciplined, knowledgeable, skilled, persuasive, determined? Are these the qualities of a good leader, or is there something more? What about kindness, empathy, approachability or being inspirational?

What is certain is that our image of what a good leader is has changed in recent times. No longer do we adhere to the concept of someone controlling things with an iron grip who sits on a pedestal created by their own ego. We now recognize that leadership is not merely the use of power by someone to get what he or she wants, neither is it a one-way relationship in which we bow down to our superiors simply because of their rank. Nowadays, a good leader is someone who is not 'superhuman', but just more 'human.'

This is where emotional intelligence comes in, which is now highly regarded as one of the most important qualities of any good leader, teacher, employer, mentor, coach or even parent. Leadership is not only about having analytical skills, a head for numbers, a loud voice or being a guardian of the rules. It is so much more than that, with those exhibiting such 'human' qualities being much more appreciated than those who shout a lot and throw their status around, expecting allegiance in return.

If you recall, EI is about having the ability to understand, manage and develop your emotions, as well as being able to understand and manage other people's feelings. It relates to how you feel about yourself and how you communicate and empathize with others to create positive outcomes for you and those you interact with. High emotional intelligence is becoming increasingly recognized as important in large organizations and those who exhibit such qualities are chosen because of their ability to deal effectively with complex social structures.

Leadership still requires authority and good leaders are not a soft touch, but being able to share a vision with the group and put their needs first creates more productive and successful results. This doesn't just apply in the workplace: great leaders can emerge in all walks of life, from being the organizer of your local hiking club to the father or mother of five children. Wherever someone is in a position where they have to lead, the more emotionally intelligent you are, the better.

Here, you can substitute the word 'leader' for 'mentor', 'coach' or any other role in which someone is expected to inspire, encourage and lead. I am not just talking about top CEOs or those of political rank. Society is broken up into millions of small cells or groups, each one focusing on a particular goal for a particular reason, with someone usually acting as a figurehead. It could be your trainer at the gym, your university professor, your life coach or your brother/sister in a family-run business. Someone is in charge and we need them to lead us. We also need to be able to follow them in order to reach an optimal outcome. If you are uninspired by your gym trainer, you may change or go to another gym. When your university professor fails to show empathy, you may drop out of his/her class, even though you like the subject. Having a life coach who doesn't seem to be helping you to progress will be a waste of money and if your elder sibling in charge of the family business doesn't communicate with you effectively, the business itself could end up folding.

Being a good leader then is not just about getting people to do things at all costs. It is about being able to control one's emotions, as well as getting along with people. Those with a low EI will find themselves constantly coming up against barriers because no one wants to follow them. Not only that: they can't sense how others feel about them and are unable to have any other perspective other than their own. This is truly not the mark of a good leader.

If you have a position which requires you to lead, think about how you do that by looking at the following statement and note which ones you strongly identify with:

1. I understand the reasons for my feelings.
2. I understand how other people's experiences affect their feelings, thoughts, and behavior.
3. I understand my leadership strengths and weaknesses.
4. I see people as good and well-intentioned.
5. I look forward to the future.
6. I can describe my feelings in detail, beyond just "happy," "sad," "angry," etc.
7. I manage stress well.
8. I focus on opportunities rather than obstacles.
9. I'm calm in the face of pressure or emotional turmoil.
10. I feel hopeful.
11. I control my impulses.
12. I'm optimistic in the face of challenging circumstances.
13. I use strong emotions, such as anger, fear, and joy appropriately.

14. I'm patient.
15. I try to understand why people behave the way they do.
16. I'm adept at managing multiple, conflicting demands.
17. I understand the viewpoints of others that are different from my own.
18. I'm flexible when situations change unexpectedly.
19. I understand how stress affects my mood and behavior.
20. I can easily adjust goals when circumstances change.
21. I can describe my emotions the moment I experience them.
22. I can shift my priorities quickly.
23. I am curious about others and listen to them attentively.
24. I strive to understand people's underlying feelings.
25. I adapt easily when a situation is uncertain or ever-changing.

These are all aspects of an emotionally intelligent leader. How well did you do? Can you relate to many of them, some of them, a few of them, or none at all? It is also a good idea to ask those within your team or group to answer the questions in relation to you. You may receive feedback that is pleasantly surprising or terribly disappointing. Whatever the results, you can use that to focus more on which aspects of your leadership skills need improving and pat yourself on the back for the skills that you have mastered.

You may have past experience of people in power coming across as tough, unapproachable and authoritarian, wielding a big stick to get things done. This stereotype is no longer wanted or appreciated, as we turn to more human-centric leaders to guide us and place our trust in. You only need to look around today to see that the great leaders of our time aren't bombastic buffoons who demand allegiance at any cost, but more down-to-earth, caring personalities who elicit respect because of their compassion and caring acts.

Social influencers may actually have more power than political rulers in our present time, especially those who seem to be selfless and committed to a just cause. They earn more respect and loyalty in the public arena simply by appealing to our recognition of basic human needs. A great example of this is David Attenborough, the broadcaster, conservationist and naturalist who broke the world record for the fastest time to reach 1 million followers when he made his recent debut on Instagram at the age of 94. Within four hours, he had obliterated the record previously held by Jennifer Aniston and only a week or so later had reached 5.8 million followers, and counting.

What is striking about this example is that if he was running for president, he would probably have a landslide victory, not because he knows anything about politics, but because he is a person of exceptional emotional intelligence who knows exactly how to communicate, inspire and produce results. Would you vote for him? There are many other examples of people much lesser known within the community who offer leadership in times of natural disasters, crises, social upheaval or to help people to rally around a cause. Those with high EQ naturally rise to the top because they appeal to the needs or desires of the followers.

A parent should also be a good leader, not only by setting a good example but by raising their children to be emotionally intelligent. I could write a separate book about good parenting but suffice to say here that EQ can be taught, and the younger a child begins to learn, the better. When we learn from an early age to process our emotions and to handle them, in all likelihood we will grow up to be natural leaders who can also empathise with others and encourage positivity instead of negativity. A child who is emotionally stunted by its parents' lack of or poor leadership will find life's challenges very difficult to overcome.

Being a good leader doesn't mean always being in a great mood or not having any problems. Greatness comes from being able to recognize that you don't feel wonderful today and that problems do exist, but having the awareness of that and finding ways to handle both effectively. Being open and willing to change, alter course, take the advice of others and be prepared to admit mistakes is also crucial to leadership, no matter what the circumstances.

An emotionally intelligent leader will be able to have a positive outcome by:

- Developing a collective set of goals and a strategic plan for achieving them.
- Instilling knowledge and the importance of the goals in others.
- Generating and maintaining enthusiasm, confidence, and optimism.
- Fostering cooperation and trust.
- Encouraging flexibility in decision making and embracing change.

To do all of the above, you should:

- Be clear about the desired goals.
- Create a vision that inspires.
- Communicate on multiple levels.
- Set a path for goal achievement.
- Share your optimism.
- Allow space for growth.

• Listen intently

Two-way communication is essential to achieve mutual trust and you can go back to the section on Better Communication to refresh your memory on how to achieve that. Instead of shouting and demanding that people follow orders, great leaders spend more time quietly listening before making suggestions. This is a skill that we can all benefit from and definitely one that empowers the individual and can earn you trust, loyalty and respect.

Being a good leader is not only about leading in the traditional sense of the word. Most of us are so exposed to a vast power bank of information, trends and knowledge that we feel we could easily do the job of many people in power or positions of authority. In fact, we even feel that most of the former are doing a pretty bad job and we all have our own opinions on the right or wrong way to do things.

As I mentioned earlier on in the book, no matter how many qualifications you may have, it doesn't necessarily mean that you can inspire others – that takes more than just academic accolades. Emotional intelligence is a skill that not all practice, but which can be acquired without having to go through university or specialized education. Managing people is not about how many degrees you have – it's about how well you can create a collaborative environment where everyone has a voice. Whether it is inspiring your pupils as a teacher or getting your local community to share your vision of a new playground, creating a dedicated team comes through being aware of their emotions, ambitions, likes and dislikes.

Using emotional intelligence, you can also have a positive impact on the group dynamic as you become aware of how emotions can be mastered for the optimum outcome. Imagine a scenario where there is discord, disputes, personality clashes and disagreements (and that could even be a normal bunch of 3rd graders or your teenage kids, never mind fully-grown adults).

Often, in a dispute, things get heated and heads lock, but by diffusing the confrontation, you can accomplish so much more. By using emotional restraint, you are leading in how to behave, carrying an olive branch that will avoid feelings of loss of face or having to back down. This is a crucial skill that can benefit all involved.

It is often said that a chain is only as strong as its weakest link. Often, that weakest link is not one of the team players or group members, but a leader who is unable to lead. Not being able to communicate, inspire, empathize and understand others is a hurdle that can be overcome if you apply emotional intelligence, beginning with yourself. I'll finish this section with a quote by the founder of emotional intelligence on leadership:

"If your emotional abilities aren't in hand, if you don't have self-awareness, if you are not able to manage your distressing emotions, if you can't have empathy and have effective relationships, then no matter how smart you are, you are not going to get very far."
— Daniel Goleman

The power of motivation and self-discipline

Is it motivation that gets someone to the gym each day, or self-discipline?

My friend Ron gets up at 5 am each day and is in the gym by 5.30. He does an hour's workout before returning home, getting changed and leaving for work at 7. That takes a lot of self-discipline, doesn't it? I asked him one day what motivates him and he told me that it has just become a habit for him now. Initially, he had started working out in order to lose weight after his ex-girlfriend told him he was fat. Ron really took that to heart and her cruel comment was enough to spur him into action. Now happily married to his current wife, he continues to stick to his exercise program, even on days when he would prefer a lie-in.

Motivation is one thing and self-disciple is quite another, but both can be instrumental in getting us to where we want to be. It doesn't have to be something physical either. Motivating ourselves to achieve greater success at work, improve our relationships with others or pursuing our goals are all things that can benefit from motivation and self-discipline.

Motivation

Let's take a look at motivation itself, and try to examine what it means, where it comes from, and how to get it.

You may feel totally unmotivated to read this book any further. If so, there could be two reasons why: firstly, you don't see any external reward (i.e., you aren't being paid to do it) or secondly, you don't see any internal reward, meaning that you don't feel the need to learn about emotional intelligence.

Simply put, if there is nothing in it for you, why bother?

Motivation comes from two sources: extrinsic influences and intrinsic desires.

Extrinsic motivation comes when we are moved to achieve a specific outcome, either for ourselves or for a greater good. It may also be a way to avoid something negative. You may be highly motivated to save up money to buy a new laptop because you need it or you could be motivated to join a community group in order to deal with the problem of excess traffic near the local school.

Intrinsic motivation is slightly different: it causes us to act in a certain way because that activity is interesting in itself, or satisfying to you. Your motivation to learn more about gardening is based on your interest in the subject and your desire to engage more productively or creatively in the activity.

Can you think of one recent example in which you were motivated extrinsically to do something, and another example of one in which you were intrinsically motivated? How did you feel about achieving your goal in either example?

What we do know is that motivation is linked to wellbeing and sense of self. As humans, our desire to attain mastery over something is highly rewarding. It nurtures our self-esteem and enriches our lives. More importantly, when the motivation is intrinsic, as opposed to extrinsic, it is even more satisfying. We are being authentic to who we are, responding to our needs and cultivating greater inner balance.

Helping out the local community may be for a good reason, but pursuing your interest in gardening will give a greater sense of personal gratification. Intrinsic motivation is critical because we need more than external rewards. We need to feel good about ourselves.

If you have ever watched a child drawing, you will notice that they are totally engrossed in what they are doing. The act itself is the motivation – the process of creating something unique. There is no reward at the end of it, only personal satisfaction. This kind of activity puts the child in what is known as the 'flow state', during which he or he is completely immersed in doing something for its own sake.

Being in such a 'flow state' is not only uplifting but also crucial in building psychological capital over time, enabling one to grow and flourish. You may be very self-disciplined at work and get through your projects on time, but if you aren't intrinsically motivated, you will not be enjoying yourself. And considering we spend a large part of our waking day at work, it's a pity if it is not bringing us any emotional growth, isn't it?

NBA players are set on winning with their team, but the act of playing the game itself is a deeply personal and satisfying activity for such athletes. When asked how they can concentrate on the game with so much noise coming from the crowd, many players report that they hardly notice it. They are so 'in the zone' that they are unaware of the yelling and cheering for much of the game and don't become aware of it until they are out on the bench. That's a great example of intrinsic motivation – can you think of another from your own life?

And don't forget – success doesn't necessarily lead to happiness. You may have just completed an award-winning bid for your company, but if your only motivation was the acquisition of a new client while you were completely disengaged when preparing the bid, the success won't bring you inner happiness. Sure, you may get a nice, fat bonus at the end of the month, but will that really make you feel good deep down, or will it simply give you more spending power? Don't get me wrong – money is not an evil in itself – but it can't buy us happiness, which I am sure you will agree on.

Self-Discipline

As you just read, motivation can be the driving force behind everything we do. It can make you jump out of the bed each morning and go for that run or propel you to working extra hard to meet your deadlines. But how long does motivation last? If you run out of steam, what can you use to keep going? That's where self-discipline comes in.

Self-discipline helps you to form habits that are in line with your needs and desires, becoming habit-forming even when you have used up all of your motivation. You may have begun that diet a few weeks ago full of enthusiasm and now feel emotionally detached from the whole idea. It is self-discipline which is going to work in your favor from now on and help you to lose those pounds.

If motivation is the reason 'why' you do something, then self-discipline is 'how' you do it.

Contrary to what you may initially think, self-discipline isn't about being hard on yourself or enlisting on a personal boot camp. It is more to do with common sense, setting priorities and thinking before acting. You don't have to give up the things that give you pleasure; neither do you need to adopt some kind of Spartan regime. It is a matter of self-control and inner strength.

Imagine that you want to cut down on your sugar intake (if you already did, well done!). It may sound like an easy task, but it is difficult to change long-term eating habits that you have been so used to. Self-disciple comes to the fore here because, without it, you may not succeed in your goal, no matter how motivated you initially feel. If you believe in the core value of your goals, you will become more confident that you can achieve them, have more self-control, be driven by logic and acquire patience.

Carol is a self-confessed chocoholic. She could easily skip lunch and dinner but binge on chocolate all day. Anyone who relates to Carol will know that too much chocolate can cause a lot of grief, from health effects like constipation to having withdrawal symptoms when going without.

Although we now know that chocolate isn't really 'addictive', it is an example of a food that can produce intense cravings, loss of control in relation to these cravings, with negative consequences when consumed to excess.

In a recent study published in the Archives of General Psychiatry, researchers at Yale University asked volunteers to fill out a questionnaire about addictive behaviour. Following that, the volunteers' brains were imaged while being able to smell, see and drink a chocolate milkshake. Those who came up as having a higher level of food addiction experienced a surge in the brain that relates to cravings and rewards. A similar pattern of brain activity can be seen in people with drug addiction.

There seems to be evidence that people, like Carol, experience psychological reactions while eating chocolate, although there is little evidence to suggest that there is a real physical addiction, unlike other controlled drugs. If you take Carol's chocolate away from her, she is likely to behave like a crazed user who needs her next fix, but it is not the same as someone who is suffering from a real physical addiction. The chocolate example merely shows us that we can use self-discipline to regulate what we do and moderate our actions. Our health may depend on it.

If you are also a 'chocoholic', try this the next time you reach for your secret stash:

• When you have a craving, pay attention to how you are feeling.
• Instead of taking the chocolate bar, delay your action for a few moments and give yourself time to 'decide' whether or not to indulge.
• If you decide to take the chocolate bar, focus on each bite slowly and extend the pleasure.
• Try to eat only half of the chocolate bar this time, and save the other half for later.
• If you decide to wait, give yourself a pat on the back

This is a very simple exercise in self-discipline. We will cover more exercises in Part Three of this book but already, you can begin to see how it doesn't have to include suffering or the absence of pleasure. On the contrary – it can be very empowering.

It's no coincidence that studies show those with greater self-control have higher self-esteem, better relationships and more optimal emotional responses. You are also more likely to feel more content, happier and satisfied with life. Think of it this way: being disciplined frees you from bad habits, an unhealthy lifestyle and poor social connections. Yes, that's right – having self-discipline can be a very liberating thing!

How athletes develop mental strength

What's your favorite sport?

Baseball, basketball, track and field, tennis? If you are an athlete yourself, you will understand a lot about the importance of mental strength. If you are a spectator, you will definitely admire athletes for their discipline and stamina.

As anyone knows, it's not easy to get to the top and athletes have to work many years to achieve and sustain their peak physical condition. We can learn something from them when it comes to self-discipline and although the aim of an athlete is to be in top physical and mental condition, we can be inspired by their techniques in our everyday life for work, family, dreams and ambitions.

Want to be the next Usain Bolt of your company?

The record-breaking sprinter is widely considered to be the greatest sprinter of all time, with 8 Olympic gold medals to his name and 11 World Championship titles. Talking about his sporting achievements in the 2016 film documentary "I Am Bolt", the sprinter commented, *"That's what I wanted people to see, the struggles, the pain, the triumph, the stress that I've been through and then have more insight also on my life."*

Let's have a look at the five traits of self-discipline:

1. Self-knowledge
Discipline means doing what is best for you, regardless of how you may be feeling. That is where self-knowledge comes in: deciding what actions reflect your goals and values. This requires a high level of emotional intelligence, where you are able to carry out self-analysis and introspection.

2. Conscious awareness

You need to be aware of what you are doing and why. It takes time to develop self-discipline and to also take note of when you are undisciplined, but practice makes perfect. The more aware you become, the better aligned you are to your goals and values.

3. Commitment

This means an internal commitment, like a vow or promise to yourself. By making a conscious decision to follow through on something, you are on the way to achieving your ends. It may seem difficult at first, but the more successful you are, the easier it becomes.

4. Courage

Yes, it takes courage to achieve your goals and self-discipline can be a scary prospect. Add to that your moods, passions and temptations and you can imagine what I mean. The desire to stay one more hour in bed, say "no" to invites for a drink and steering your own course require a warrior mentality.

5. Internal coaching

You are your best coach and the only one who can talk you into or out of action. By telling yourself, "you can do it", you are reaffirming confidence in your abilities. When that little voice in your head tells you it is OK not to bother today, be the bigger voice, who says that the bother is always worth the effort.

Finally, it's important to remember that most successful athletes don't always think about winning at the time of competing. Many prefer to have a clear mindset, during which they focus on the moment and not the finish line, the last whistle or the cup final. One step at a time and focusing on the "now" can be the most empowering mindset to have.

How failure can make you a better person

Do you come from the school of hard knocks? Or perhaps you graduated from the University of Life.

In 1918, an item appeared in the Peninsula Enterprise newspaper with the following words: *"School of Hard Knocks. Much of our education is to be obtained only in the school of hard knocks. There is no age limit and the sooner we are graduated, the better for us."*

The two idioms I mentioned above are often used by people who have undergone negative experiences in their life and have gone on to overcome them. Although originally used in reference to education, both now have more general meanings and are typically used by someone claiming a level of wisdom acquired by life experience which could be seen as having at least equal merit to academic knowledge.

Building resilience through hardship may be ok if you sign up for the Marine Corps, but no one should have to go through that in order to find happiness. Unfortunately, life is full of setbacks and even though they aren't usually life-threatening, the sense of failure can feel devastating. Failing to overcome the challenges that we face doesn't make us a weak person though. Neither does one failure reflect on our overall worth as a valuable member of the community.

Unfortunately, we live in a society where failure is not looked upon kindly and in which people are usually measured by their success. This adds to the personal struggle that we may have with our failings, under-achievements and inability to materialize our dreams. Learning how to deal with those failures and getting back on the horse is a 'must' if we want to make the most of life, and acquiring emotional intelligence can help us to do that.

I am sure that you have beaten yourself up more than once about a 'failure' in your life. Well, here's a little secret: everyone fails before they succeed. Going back to our friend Usain Bolt in the previous section, we never learn about the sacrifices he has had to make or the stress that he has been under throughout his career. Bolt failed to qualify in the men's 200-meter heats at the 2004 Olympics due to an injury but bounced back in 2008 to break the world record in the 100 meters sprint. For athletes like Bolt, there is no time to dwell on failures as they are always looking ahead to their next win.

It's time to stop looking at failure as something negative. If we had no sense of what it means to fail, how would we measure success? If you fail a math test, it is probably because you didn't study enough and, as testing is one means of seeing how much someone knows about a subject, you can hardly expect to pass if you have gaps in your knowledge, right? If you fail at something more personal, like meeting a deadline you have set yourself to finish a project by Friday, you are letting yourself down. Failure only becomes a problem when it is frequent and avoidable, or when we take it to heart and allow it to affect our self-worth and esteem.

I want you to think about failure for a moment:

- What have you failed at in life?
- How did it affect you?
- Does it have any impact on your life now?
- What did you learn from it?

The last question is the most important because failure is unavoidable; it's how we deal with it that matters most. The truth is that failure is never the end of the road. It is simply a slow-bump that shows us where we need to make more effort in order to get the results that we desire.

With the push in society to be high-achiever, failure is often seen as the worst scenario and no one likes a loser. That is all very unrealistic in reality, but it can get under our skin and make us feel completely incapable. Sitting in a negative place may be the best place to begin assessing what is going on with you, and why you aren't able to achieve your goals.

Dusting yourself down and forging ahead without taking a minute to consider what went wrong means that you are even more likely to make the same mistakes in the future. Emotionally intelligent people linger on their failures for a while, before they start moving on again. Dealing with the leaking hole now will prevent you from having to face an even bigger leak further down the road.

Failure can have different effects on different people – it can make some give up, while others become more determined to go on. It is a potent force either way and depending on how you deal with it will determine how you face knock-backs in the future. The opposite of failure is success, which triggers reactions in certain parts of our brain associated with our overall learning and growth capabilities. To that extent, the age-old phrase, "We learn from our mistakes" really is true.

A lot of it depends on the mindset that you are already carrying with you. If you have what is known as a 'growth mindset', an enhanced focus state is triggered after failing a task, forcing you to learn and improve. If you have a 'fixed mindset', you will show little improvement after facing failure. Research has shown that the neuroplasticity of the brain changes in people with a 'growth mindset', with neurons firing, growing, and forming new connections.

It's similar to doing cryptic crosswords. If you are an absolute beginner, you may get stuck, unable to find the right words because you don't understand the way the clues are presented. For example, the clue to 53 down maybe: sweet stall (5 letters). This will make absolutely no sense to you if you are not used to the way in which cryptic crosswords play on words. Would you be surprised to learn that the answer to this clue is the word fudge? I'll just leave that there for you to think about...

If you keep at it, you will begin to understand the way that the clues are worded, and what type of answers they relate to. It takes practise, but the longer you keep at it, the better you get, because your brain has 'understood' what's needed. It's had a kind of mini growth spurt at a neuro-level. If you give in at the first attempt, no growth is detected in your brain, as you never enter into that crucial focused state of learning.

Other research has proposed that there are two areas in the prefrontal cortex responsible for the fear of failure and the lure of success. This gives credence to what psychologists call the risk and reward debate, which occurs when we have to make a decision. It could be linked to the basic need for survival, in which failure was a useful tool in learning and strengthening the species, a bit like trial and error.

Whatever researchers are saying, the fact is that no one likes to fail, right? Whether you fail a test, an exam, an interview, a marriage or a life goal, it really sucks to feel that you weren't successful. No doubt you will go through a series of negative thoughts and emotions, which will affect not only you but also those around you. Nipping that negativity in the bud is crucial because the impact on your life otherwise can be very damaging.

Here are a few of the ways in which not handling failure correctly can deprive you of leading a fulfilling life:

1. Failure makes your goals seem less attainable by distorting your mindset. Your goals may not have changed, but your perception of them has. It will seem like someone has moved the goalposts.

2. Failure also distorts your perception of your abilities. Suddenly, you don't feel good enough to achieve anything and will view yourself as being weaker than you actually are. You are a loser.

3. Failure makes you feel helpless. It's as if someone or something has wounded you emotionally, and you just can't pick yourself up. By telling you that you won't succeed, your mind is protecting itself from further pain, but this also means that you won't make any future attempts at success. Why bother?

4. It only takes one failure to develop an unconscious 'fear of failure'. Instead of focusing on future success, you are now afraid of any future failures and will avoid striving to achieve your goals. Better safe than sorry, right?

5. This fear of failure can also make you shoot yourself in the foot, creating excuses and scenarios to explain why you are likely to fail. It can even lead to developing psychosomatic symptoms like headaches or stomach upsets when the time comes to take action. Excuses, excuses...

6. If you are a parent and have a fear of failure, it is likely that you will pass this on unwittingly to your children. By overreacting to any of

their failures or withdrawing from them emotionally, you are unconsciously teaching them that failure is unacceptable. Like father, like son...

7. Needless to say, the pressure to succeed can increase anxiety and even a sense of choking. This happens because you are forcing your brain to overthink something that it does naturally, throwing it into a state of confusion and malfunction. The system breaks down.

8. Crash diets and bad eating habits deprive the brain of glucose, which it needs to operate our cognitive functions such as concentration, decision-making and willpower. Unable to think straight, motivation is reduced and our willpower diminishes. Binging doesn't help.

As I mentioned above, some life failures may be more important than others. Failing to get the washing in before it rains is no big deal in the overall scheme of things. But failing to pass an important academic exam may have lasting implications for your career. Feeling that you failed to make a personal relationship work can also seriously damage your self-esteem and confidence.

It may be easier to see that not all failures are the same, and we can separate them into three different kinds.

First of all, there are preventable failures, which basically means that you had enough information and the ability to avoid something, but didn't. It could be something like getting a bad grade for an exam because you didn't study enough, or having a row with your best friend because you were late turning up for a dinner. If you feel bad when something like this happens, you should.

Secondly, there are complex failures, which occur when we know what needs to be done, but a combination of personal or external factors come together to produce failure. Often, this kind of failure is unavoidable, making it difficult to attribute blame. Running a new start-up may include trying to manage many factors all at once, and the breakdown of one aspect can throw a spanner in the works. These types of failure are not necessarily bad – they could point out what needs correcting in order to achieve future success.

Finally, we can talk about emotional failure, which has to do with something very personal in our life. It could be to do with unsuccessful relationships or a lifelong goal that we were unable to achieve. Such failures can induce real pain and heartache, knocking us back and negating any other successes we have ever had in life. The main problem here is that we make it too personal.

If you have recently experienced any of the above, you may still be licking your wounds and wondering what went wrong. It's important to recognize and accept your emotions instead of minimizing them. Giving yourself some time to hurt is OK, but blaming yourself long after the event is counter-productive in the long-term.

When you fail at something, that doesn't make you a failure. It's not personal – you will continue to be you. By all means, spend some time looking at your mistakes and make a promise to yourself to avoid them in the future, but think of it as a lesson, not a punishment. Categorizing yourself as either a failure or a success is not a healthy perspective to have of your own identity.

Worried about what people will say? Sometimes, our sense of failure is exaggerated by what we believe others will think of us or how they will judge us. After all, who doesn't recall feeling the wrath of their parents on producing a bad report card? Status anxiety is something that I have already touched on previously and what is important is being your own critic, rather than feeling that you are on trial, often by people who hardly know you.

Owning up to your mistakes and being accountable is a brave thing to do. Instead of blaming someone or something else, thinking of ways in which you could have improved your performance or your actions is more productive. Did you really work hard enough to deserve that promotion? Did you listen enough to your partner's complaints? These are the kinds of questions which will help you to achieve clarity, but they require honest answers.

Finally, think of failure as a chance to improve. It is one of life's lessons and never signifies the end of the world. By working out what went wrong, you are better prepared next time around. Self-forgiveness and self-compassion are important too. Chastising yourself over and over again will eventually wear you down while being kind to yourself will make overcoming failure a much easier process.

Bringing emotional intelligence to the workplace

Can you be emotionally intelligent in a work environment?

Work is just work, right? You get up each day, commute to your place of work, do your thing, get on well with colleagues and maybe set on going even further in your career. And then you go home and have your personal life, which is when you can enjoy your free time. But did you count up how many hours you spend at work each week, month or year? It's an enormous chunk of your life, and if you are not in an environment which is conducive to overall employee wellness, work can eventually make you sick.

I am not talking about physical tiredness, although that is an important element of work which can take its toll. I am referring to the psychological stresses and strains of spending at least 8 hours a day in a setting which may be toxic, mismanaged, harsh, isolating and even unbearable. Ask yourself: do any of these negative points resonate with you and your job?

Company culture is slowly catching up with our expectations of the workplace being a healthy environment in which we deserve to be treated with respect and understanding. No longer is it acceptable for us to be slaves to some kind of corporate feudalism in which our performance is measured by how robotic we can be – now we have robots to do that.

Wherever you work and in whatever capacity, you expect to be treated with fairness, dignity and to be remunerated accordingly. Unfortunately, you may be subject to a supervisor or employer who doesn't share your expectations, which can cause you to actually hate your job. But hope is not lost, because more and more firms are beginning to recognize that those employees with high levels of emotional intelligence are much more valuable assets to the company than those stuck in the past with a low EQ.

In fact, many employers are now putting a premium on hiring employers who are able to understand and control their emotions, people who can relate to others and communicate well. As long as they have the threshold experience, IQ and technical skills needed, having the bonus of being emotionally intelligent makes that candidate a much more favorable option for employers.

Recruiters have embedded this demand into their list of suitable candidates for positions and are now looking for more than just skills on paper. They are also looking for the signs of emotional intelligence, which may come in the form of an assessment test, or via questions such as; "How did you deal with a particular challenge in the past?" The way you respond will give them an idea of how emotionally intelligent you are.

A World Economic Forum survey taken in 2018 found that EQ was one of the 10 most in-demand skills by employers. Clearly, having the technical skills is not enough anymore and strong collaboration and social skills are now deemed to be essential. Don't be surprised therefore if you are posed questions such as the following on your next job interview:

1. Describe a time you were given critical feedback.
2. Describe a time when you had to have a difficult conversation.
3. Describe a time when there was tension or conflict on a team.
4. Describe a time a change was instituted that you didn't agree with.
5. Describe a time when you had to come up with a creative solution under pressure.
6. Describe a time you made a mistake.

These are all directed at measuring your emotional intelligence. After reaching this point in the book, you should be an expert on understanding the significance of these questions. When talking about the time you received critical feedback or an occasion on which you made a mistake, the interviewer isn't interested in the details, but in how you handled the situation. Did you respond in a manner that exhibits emotional intelligence or did you become defensive, make the same mistake again, have a blow-up or quit? I think you know what the correct answer should be.

We talked in the last section about emotional intelligence and leadership. You can apply all of the points we discussed to the workplace, where leadership or management is a crucial position within any successful enterprise. So what is the essence of an emotionally intelligent group leader, line-manager, department head or CEO? If we go back to the standard definition of someone who is aware of their emotions and able to regulate them, has the internal motivation, empathy and great social skills, then we can translate those into the following:

• A team player_– Someone who works for the greater good of their team and company. They appreciate being embraced but don't rely on that to elevate their self-esteem.
• Positive and down to earth – They take work in their stride and aren't easily hassled, but they are realistic and pay attention to issues that cause problems.
• Focused – They are able to leave their personal issues at the door when they come to work and focus on the job at hand.
• Accountable – They don't make excuses or blame others when mistakes

happen. They own up to the problem and learn from the experience.

- Confident – They're not afraid of failure or embarrassment and that doesn't prevent them from trying out new ideas and asking questions.
- Ego free – They have confidence but are not arrogant or cocky.
- Solve disputes – They are peacemakers without losing dignity and stay level-headed when facing challenges.
- Inspiring – They raise people up instead of putting them down and inspire others to do the same.

As the world around us continues to be in a constant state of flux and uncertainty, having an emotionally intelligent leader or team member is an invaluable asset for any company. If you are an employer, recruiting those with a high level of emotional intelligence will definitely bring many positives to your company. It is linked to higher job satisfaction both for those with a high EQ, as well as employees who work or are managed by someone with a high EQ. That is strongly associated with job performance, increased productivity and a better working environment.

How does that translate in real terms? Let's look at it this way:

1. An upset employee finds a compassionate ear
A person with a high EQ will notice that something is up with his/her colleague and offer compassion and understanding. Those with a low EQ will come across as mean and uncaring.

2. People pay more attention to each other in meetings
Emotionally intelligent managers or employees allow others to speak and listen attentively without interrupting. Meetings at which no one dares speak are a complete waste of time.

3. People express themselves openly
A person with a high EQ is comfortable about speaking up as well as listening to others express their own opinions. Those with low emotional intelligence may simply keep all emotions and opinions to themselves or give vent in office gossip.

4. Change is welcomed
Employees with high emotional intelligence are likely to handle change well and to apply the changes in earnest. Those resistant to change make less effort to adjust and may even sabotage changes.

5. Flexibility
A company that exhibits flexibility and understanding of the complex lives

of its workforce members is probably run by a high EQ culture with managers who acknowledge that people have different needs. The alternative is boredom and disinterest.

6. Creativity is welcomed
Workplaces that allow their employees to be creative and innovative are high EQ. When thinking outside the box is welcomed, it can generate a much healthier and productive workforce. Companies that insist on rigid policies and regulations leave little room for creativity.

7. People meet out of work time
A good sign of emotional intelligence in the workplace is when members socialize outside of the workplace and deepen their bonds. Emotionally intelligent colleagues and managers tend to get along with others and see the value in investing their time and energy in workplace relationships.

While employing those who exhibit emotional intelligence is now recognized as an essential recruitment requirement, those higher up in the company hierarchy will also do well to develop a culture of emotional intelligence in the workplace. Having great managers is just as important as having a great team, and only together can great results be achieved.

PART THREE

10 LIFE HACKS TO A NEW YOU

#1 Dealing with the past and forgiving others

It's time to move on.

So far in this book, we have looked at different aspects of emotional intelligence and talked about the benefits of being in touch with our emotions. We have also discussed ways in which qualities like self-esteem and motivation play an important role in our overall success and happiness. I hope that you now have a greater understanding of the basic foundations of your human experience and are ready to start rebuilding a new you. That begins with living in the moment.

The magic suitcase

Imagine that from the age of one, someone starts packing you a magic suitcase, filling it with events, memories and emotions as you grow up. By the time you reach seven or thereabouts, you are able to pack it yourself and continue to do so up until adulthood. You take it everywhere with you and the reason that it is a magic suitcase is because no matter how much you pack into it, it always remains the same size.

What you have noticed recently though is that it seems to be getting so heavy that you are struggling to carry it around with you. One day you feel that it is just weighing you down and you are tired of lugging this battered old baggage on your back. It's time to open it and lighten the load. As you do, you find millions and millions of things inside that have absolutely no relevance to your life today and wonder to yourself, "Why on earth am I still carrying this stuff around with me in my suitcase?"

As soon as you do that, the item that you picked up from when you were 2 or 15 or 21 year's old simply disappears - that's the magic suitcase.

We are all carrying a magic suitcase around with us. Some of us may have lost the key to open it, some are afraid to do so, and others might even try to hide it under the bed or in the closet. But make no mistake about it – each and every one of us has been filling up a magic suitcase since before we can even remember.

You get the analogy for life, right?

So how do we deal with the past and forgive others?

Well, we have to begin by looking at our present and forgiving ourselves first. That means getting rid of excess baggage, which is not only cumbersome but also keeps us stuck at check-in and unable to fly.

Just a memory

Our magic suitcase is packed with memories; some good and some bad. You can and should keep the good ones. Memory is a funny thing – it gives us certainty about who we are. It is part of our personal identity and the sum of all our parts. Without it, who would we be?

My mother suffered from Alzheimer's in later life and although it began with small memory lapses and confusion, as the disease severely progressed, she had no recollection of who I or my siblings were. In fact, she had no recollection of who she was herself. While painful for us to witness and frustrating no doubt at times for my mother, in general, she seemed content. She had lost that ability to recall memories and was only temporarily aware of her surroundings from moment to moment.

For us who are healthy and living an active life, we need the past because it gives us certainty about who we are and where we are going. Certainty is one of the most basic human needs and is part of our survival skills. It helps us to avoid pain and pursue comfort; it gives us the courage to try new things and to progress. We cling onto the past because it makes us feel safe, even if some of our past experiences were very damaging ones. They simply become our point of reference, our ground zero.

The problem occurs when we link emotions to past events and allow those emotions to surface whenever a similar event occurs in our present. If you fell off a pony when you were a kid and grazed your knee, does that mean that you should never get on a horse again? If someone told you at 18 that you would never make anything of yourself, does that mean that you should never try to achieve your goals? Of course, the logical answer to both questions is no. But what happens is that sometimes we carry those emotions of pain, rejection or even emotional abuse around with us, and they become markers of who we think we are.

But, they are just memories.

Live in the now

There is no such thing as the past. There is only this moment – the present, the now. Your memories are remnants of a past that has nothing to do with your present situation. The anger you may feel now about a past incident is weighing you down and you need to release it. Of course, you have a history and recall moments from that history, but recalling the negative ones over and over again in your mind is self-destructive. And apart from that, they serve absolutely no purpose whatsoever.

A memory is simply a thought that you conjure up in your mind. It's not part of your DNA and has no power other than that which you give to it. When you have an emotional reaction to some thoughts, you are reinforcing their influence over you, which can be harmful to your wellbeing and affect your relationships with others. If you had some kind of trauma in your childhood, that aroused sense of fear or pain may distort your idea of what healthy relationships are, leading you to provoke drama and conflict in your relationships today.

It's time to let go of those painful experiences and leave them where they belong – in the past.

Step 1 Closure
- Often, things come up from the past because we have never fully put them to rest. We may torment ourselves with grief or attempt to understand what went wrong without success. At the end of the day, it is the impact of an unfinished event that stays with us, and the facts are secondary.
- If you are still upset with your ex, write down all the things that you wanted to say to them, just to get it out of your head. By getting how you feel out of your system through expressing it, your anger, pain or sadness will eventually begin to fade.

Step 2 Post-traumatic stress
- Any traumatic experience will cause your brain to push that event to the non-verbal part of its function because it is too difficult to confront. It

could be a minor trauma such as a car accident, or something more serious like abuse or war. Those raw images play out like a silent movie in your mind, causing you to have flashbacks, perhaps hypervigilance, and a sense of fear.

- If this is the case, please consider seeking professional help and learn how new techniques and therapies can restore calm in your life. There is no need to let trauma continue to ruin your happiness.

Step 3 Disturbed sleep

- It seems as if our brain waits for the moment we are ready to sleep to bring up all of those painful past memories. Lying in bed thinking about them is like letting a bull into a china shop – it will go on the rampage. Although it is good to reflect on the events of the day, restrict yourself to that alone and not what happened five or ten years ago.

- Relaxing before you go to sleep is imperative, and that means no screen time for at least one hour prior, disabling your cell phone notifications, and ensuring a calm space.

Step 4 Get to the bottom of things

- If you have unresolved issues with things that happened in the past, such as your parents' divorce, they may prevent you from being successful in your own relationships. It is important to know that you do not need to follow the same pattern of behavior as your parents and that you are an autonomous person.

- Speak to your mother or father and ask them about their divorce. Often, our memories are so wrapped up in strong emotions that we never get to the facts. Once you can join the dots, it may be easier to come to terms with what happened and to move on in your life.

Step 5 Disarm the past

- Once you neutralize your story, it will lose its power over you. The point is not to negate your past or pretend that it didn't happen, both of which are impossible to do anyway. Don't try to ignore how you feel about it, which can lead to suppressed anxiety and stress. You shouldn't expect an apology or acknowledgement from anyone concerned or wait for time to heal, because that may take too long. What you can do is change your reaction to what happened.

- When you update the narrative about your past, especially childhood memories, you can create a more complete picture from an adult perspective. This will give you a better sense of what is in the past and what to choose for your future. Only keep in your magic suitcase what is useful to you now and trash the rest.

Can you forgive?

We forgive our children when they do something 'wrong' and are capable of showing great compassion to others who have inadvertently hurt us. You will have even heard stories of the families of victims forgiving their killers, or of individuals granting forgiveness to perpetrators of horrific war crimes.

What we see here is people who've experienced horrific pain, making a conscious decision to forgive.

I say decision because that is exactly what forgiveness is.

It is the decision to accept that something happened but not allowing it to chain you to the past. It is not about forgetting, making friends with the person who has wronged you or saying what happened is OK. It is the decision to free yourself of loss, pain or anger.

We all have the capacity to forgive and it is that which lays the foundation for our relationships. You may be angry at your partner for turning up late for dinner, but that anger soon fades away after a while. When we look at the incident in context and the reasons for the lateness, it is usually the case that holding on to anger is pointless and outweighs the 'crime'.

It is not easy to forgive someone, but in reality, you should begin by liberating yourself from the negative feelings associated with the culprit and past events. Research has shown that forgiveness is a powerful human act that releases us from anger, resentment and vengeful feelings, all of which can have a detrimental impact on our lives.

A young woman was suffering from depression and sought the help of a therapist. During the sessions, the woman talked a lot about her traumatic childhood upbringing with an alcoholic father, whom she felt unable to forgive. Although he had passed away several years earlier, she had not even been able to bring herself to attend his funeral. Full of anger and resentment for him, she was allowing her father to severely impact her life even now.

Over time and with careful counselling, the woman was able to take several steps towards relieving herself of this emotional burden, which was seriously impacting her relationship with her own husband. She learnt to accept her past, not to forget it. Moreover, she was able to come to terms with how she had been plagued by many other feelings, such as guilt, shame and inability to trust others.

One of the breakthrough moments came when the therapist helped her to see that she did not need to be a victim of someone else's behaviour (in this case, her father). It was up to her to reclaim herself and to allow for self-forgiveness. Once she was able to do that, her father stopped having a hold on her present and she was on the path to overcoming her depression.

How to forgive

Forgiveness is a process that involves the voluntary, internal process of letting go of feelings and thoughts of resentment, bitterness and anger. It removes the need for vengeance or retribution toward someone we believe has wronged us, including ourselves. Some people are naturally more forgiving than others, but we are all capable of doing so. It just takes time.

- If you are stuck in a cycle of anger, bitterness and a thirst for vengeance against someone, take some time out to look at how these negative feelings are upsetting your wellbeing. Is it really worth it? I am not advocating that you forget or dismiss wrongdoings – I am asking you to have self-compassion. Any negative emotions about external factors ultimately affect you internally and can cause ill health, mental conditions and lack of optimism for the future. Ask yourself if this is how you want to live your life.

- Making a willful decision to forgive someone is achievable, but may still leave you with residues of pain or hurt. You may decide to forgive someone who betrayed you but are still left with a feeling of mistrust, which can affect any future relationships. Once you see the act as an isolated case carried out by a specific person, you can quarantine it off from your life. The betrayal wasn't about you and it has no power over your next relationship.

- Emotional forgiveness comes when your negative emotions such as resentment and vengefulness are substituted by positive emotions like empathy, compassion, sympathy and altruistic love. This is perhaps the most difficult kind of forgiveness to attain, and I get that. This needs a shift, not so much in how we view things but requires a real emotional transformation. How can you possibly feel empathy for someone who consciously hurt you deeply, or carried out a grave injustice against you?

If you feel that you are unable to forgive someone, I want you to answer this question: Why is it so important for you to hold on to those feelings of anger, pain and resentment?
Spend some time reflecting on your response and think about how much your 'inability' to forgive is affecting your wellbeing. Hopefully, if you think long enough about it, you will come to the conclusion that the decision not

to forgive brings a toxic element to your life that you yourself are perpetuating. If you are ready to remove that and move on, here are 5 steps to help you do so:

1. Think about the incident that caused you pain or anger. Accept that it happened. Acknowledge how it made you feel and react and how you were affected.

2. Separate yourself from the incident and instead of seeing yourself as a victim, realize that you were a recipient of an external action carried out by someone else. It didn't happen 'because' of you.

3. Consider how you have grown as a result of what happened. What have you learned about yourself, your needs and your boundaries?

4. Think about the perpetrator, who is flawed, just as we all are. Consider his or her actions as occurring within a flawed framework of behaviour. Don't attempt to justify their actions, just see them in context.

5. Express forgiveness in your own way, by saying out loud, "I forgive you", or by writing the phrase down. You do not need to tell the perpetrator so unless you feel that it will bring further closure.

The young woman visiting the therapist reached the point where she was able to emotionally forgive her alcoholic father, by concluding that he must have been a deeply unhappy man who drank to escape his own demons. She has not forgotten his outbursts but does not blame him any more. She accepts what happened and who he was but no longer allows him to play a negative role in her life and has released the pain she was carrying around with her for so many years.

#2 Freeing yourself from people's opinions

Why do you care what other people think of you?

Is it because you seek acceptance, acknowledgement, praise or recognition? Maybe you just want to avoid rejection, criticism or feeling like an outsider. There could be other reasons, but what matters is to ask yourself why.

It may seem quite obvious at first glance – everyone wants to feel that they fit in with their peers, share similar outlooks and are basically on the same team. No one wants to stick out and be seen as 'different', right? The problem begins when what people think of you becomes restrictive and makes you feel lesser than you are, stunting your potential for growth, and that's a common occurrence.

Our craving for social approval begins on day one, from our parents, our friends and teachers, our peers and colleagues, and even those who we hardly know. This primordial need to belong to 'the group' is wired into our brain and ostracisation used to have dire consequences, as you can imagine. Early humans needed the group dynamic to survive and loners didn't have much chance of that in comparison. So what other people thought of you would have obviously mattered immensely then.

It's still important to us nowadays but paying too much attention to other people's opinions means that you are paying less attention to your own beliefs and value judgements. This harms your potential to lead a fulfilling life. And ignoring other people's opinions is not a life-threatening risk anymore. You are not going to be cast out of society and left to fend for yourself just because you don't agree with your peers on the best time to plant tulip bulbs in your garden, and neither your survival nor theirs depends on it!

What many of us do experience is the fear of being criticised, ridiculed or rejected so instead of standing up for ourselves, we will go along with what others say, even if we disagree. This has reached extreme proportions for some, with the need to be accepted and the fear of rejection dominating the whole arena of their social media life. Each time you post a carefully filtered and curated shot of yourself, you are seeking the approval of your peers, and we know how destructive to our self-esteem negative feedback can be.

Escaping this cycle of virtual perfection and crowd-pleasing isn't easy. Neither is wanting to please your wife, boss, friends or neighbours for fear of criticism, rejection or even just gossip behind your back. What other people say and think about you matters, right?

Actually, wrong!

The only thing that matters is how we view ourselves and once we lose that inner balance, we are on topsy-turvy terrain. Emotional intelligence is the ability to acknowledge our strengths and weaknesses, to stand by our decisions and to have a self-image grounded on our expectations, not someone else's. Only when you have that strong inner awareness of yourself can you reach your potential, achieve your dreams and forge lasting and meaningful relationships. So how do you get to that point?

1. <u>Your life is yours and doesn't belong to anyone else.</u> Doing what you believe to be right is no one else's business. You are entitled to your opinions and choices and are the only one qualified to approve of them.

2. Your opinion of others is your business, so keep it that way. Just as you don't want to be criticized, don't make assumptions about others, or try to force your opinions onto them. Respect for others will earn you mutual respect.

3. Only you know what is best for you, and that includes learning from your mistakes and constantly trying to improve. By taking responsibility for yourself, you are maturing and deepening your sense of self-worth, and there can be nothing more satisfying than that.

4. What's good for the goose isn't always good for the gander. Your mate may have a great perspective on life, but that doesn't mean that you have to forsake your own just to stay together. Being your own person is more important than going along with someone else's life view.

5. If every explorer listened to their peers, no one would have reached Mount Everest or discovered Tasmania! Worrying about what other people will think can seriously curtail your dreams and when it comes to putting yourself on the line, you will back out. Do you really want that to happen?

6. You are accountable for your decisions, good or bad. You can take someone's advice or not, but whatever you do, the outcome is your responsibility, so own it. Whether you make the right decision or not, it's your call, and will avoid blame or regret after the event.

7. People change their mind on a regular basis, which is completely natural. One day your boss may think you are an incompetent idiot and the next praise you for a great job, so don't judge yourself by other people's criteria – use your own instead.

8. Life is too short to worry about what other people think. You will never be able to satisfy everybody, conform to every standard or agree with everyone you meet. Focus on what matters to you and be honest with yourself – you are your best critic.

On a closing note, being bombastic, inflexible and defensive in the face of criticism are not advised. Neither is ignoring the advice of friends to hand over your car keys when you have had one drink too many. Sometimes, other people's opinions do count and acquiring the wisdom to know when that is the case is equally important.

#3 Dealing with destructive emotions

Why are you so angry?

It's a normal day, just like any other. You set off for work and get stuck in the early morning traffic. You spill your coffee when you get to the office all over your keyboard and, to top it off, you just learn that a colleague has called in sick so you will have to handle her workload. Who wouldn't be seething by now?

All justifiable reasons to be angry, you may say. But, are they really? Maybe your anger is an over-reaction to non-significant events and the real issue is why you feel so angry in the first place. Any negative emotion you experience has negative effects, both on you and those around you. Whether it is rage, fear, envy or hate, negative emotions are destructive because they can make you lose control and produce harmful results.

Destructive emotions also build up inside us and can often push aside more healing emotions such as compassion, empathy and love. If you allow the former to build up over a long period of time, you are creating a monster and the bigger it is, the more difficult it will be to control it.

By accessing your emotional intelligence, you can begin to see the underlying causes of negative emotions and learn how to control them before they get out of hand. If you stop for one moment to look at the way you are feeling, you may not like what you see, but facing it is a way to deal with it effectively.

If you suffer from road rage, imagine how aggressive you appear to other drivers. When you spill your coffee, what frame of mind does that put you in? When you are seething with anger at your colleague for calling in sick, how does that affect the work dynamic? And at the end of the day, what are those negative emotions doing to you internally?

Self-destruction

Powerful emotions like anger or rage are potentially the most self-destructive. You may not recognize the signs that they are taking over, but it is like feeding that growing giant, which can wreak havoc on your emotional and physical wellbeing. Those churning knots in your stomach and the desire to scream, or throw something against the wall are all signs that you are not responding well to events in your life.

The fear factor

Fear is a powerful and paralyzing emotion that prevents you from pursuing your goals and establishing strong connections with others. It can become a bullying tyrant that causes you to worry about things that haven't even happened yet. Fear can cause anxiety, which is another disempowering emotion that can completely take over your life if you let it. It can prevent you from eating, sleeping, concentrating, interacting with others and avoiding any situations that you think will make you fearful. Breaking the cycle is a 'must'.

Taking control

Being able to control your emotions doesn't mean suppressing them or ignoring them. The next time you experience things like fear, sadness, rage, take a minute to look at what is happening to you and ask yourself the following questions:

- What am I feeling?
- Why am I feeling it?
- What would make me feel better in this situation?
- What is a healthy way to express how I'm feeling?

Catching yourself at that moment can divert your negative reactions and give you an insight into what is really going on with you. Blaming something or someone for your negative emotions is a cop-out – it is you that is in control of your feelings. Expressing how you feel to others in a calm way is much more likely to diffuse any situation and clear the air too.

Apart from the negative impact on your health and wellbeing, negative emotions can cause you to say and do things that you wouldn't normally do. How often have you said things in anger or out of spite that you later came to regret? How many times have you lashed out at a loved one because you couldn't control your temper or because you felt hurt by something they said or did?

When emotions become destructive, they can cause serious damage, lead you to make bad decisions, act irrationally and even be a danger to yourself or others. Hence, tread carefully.

Managing your anger

Denying your reaction or trying to justify it only pushes that feeling deeper into your inner core, because you aren't resolving those negative emotions and instead, you become a tinderbox, ready to explode at the next available incident. Watch out for those signs that you are about to blow a fuse:

- Ranting and raving
- Making sarcastic or nasty comments
- Suffering from stomach, back, neck and head pains
- Having aggressive thoughts
- Feeling that you may induce a physical altercation
- Experiencing a choking sensation

Feelings of anger can be triggered by many things, but if you feel permanently angry, it could be as a result of serious trauma or an underlying medical condition. Here, I am talking about fits of anger that occur frequently, which may be ruining your relationships and your inner sense of balance. There are different types of anger too, so it's useful to look at which kind you are experiencing to learn how to deal with it.

- Are you angry about injustice in the world and the destruction of the environment, violations of human rights, the rise in crime or abuses of power? This kind of anger may be justified in the short term, and inspire you to become more active for a cause of your choice. However, feeling constantly angry at the world can be self-destructive so don't dwell too much on the negatives and balance your life with positive things as much as possible.

- Do you get annoyed easily by daily frustrations such as noisy neighbors, traffic, bad coffee, lazy workmates? Chill out – putting things into perspective will reduce your stress level. Avoid focussing on what irritates you and don't internalize what other people say or do. Some problems in life are not problems at all, and reasonable solutions can always be found.

- Do you often feel frustrated and suffer from temper tantrums? Are you a screaming toddler stamping the ground until you get what you want? This emotional reaction is linked to your emotional maturity and could originate in your childhood and continue to plague you in adulthood. Ask that child within you what they really want and listen to their answer. It may reveal a lot more about your behavior than you think.

- Do you feel like punching your boss? The thought may cross your mind, but acting aggressively can cause very serious problems, not to mention have legal implications. Aggression is a poor substitute for rational thinking, tact and diplomacy. It relies on dominance, intimidation, manipulation or control and can turn into bullying, oppression, violence and emotional abuse. Is that the person you want to be?

If you are experiencing any kind of anger, you need to look inside yourself and recognize what you are feeling: fear, insecurity, low self-esteem and inadequacy are just some of the things you may find lying just under the surface. You could also benefit from professional help to deal with these issues so please begin today to address any destructive tendencies that you feel.

It is possible to manage your anger successfully by acquiring self-awareness, developing a desire to learn and grow, and a willingness to improve your relationships. And don't forget self-compassion: understanding your personal history and emotions will give you the tools to be kind to yourself and those around you.

#4 Understanding emotions in others

Do you understand how I feel?

How many times have you been asked that question by someone you know? Probably hundreds of times. Your automatic answer is probably to say, "Yes, of course, I understand how you feel", even when you don't. The good thing is that you realize how important it is to make the other person feel that you are with them, which is a sign of emotional intelligence in the making.

One of the key aspects of emotional intelligence is your ability to understand the emotions of others and to be able to empathise with them. These are not skills that come naturally to all of us, and having a lack of them can prevent you from connecting with people and finding solutions to conflicts or differences.

I very much doubt that most of us can fully understand exactly how another person feels, often because they don't or cannot express it well enough. Being able to articulate your feelings isn't easy and many of us try to hide them, which can make communication a bit of hit and miss. But learning how to understand and empathize with others is one of the most useful life hacks that you can acquire.

If you recall, most successful leaders exhibit high levels of emotional intelligence, which includes the ability to listen well, express clearly and gain the support of their team members. Think about it: if your boss never has time for you, never listens to your suggestions and puts you down frequently, he isn't going to earn your respect, is he? Having no idea of your concerns or feelings isn't going to help you establish a deeper bond with your supervisor or head of department. You will be unhappy, unproductive and probably looking for the next job opening in a rival firm.

This kind of social intelligence comes from having self-awareness first and foremost, which then leads you to communicate well and to form healthy relationships. It's never too late to learn and by reading people's emotions, you will also gain a lot of insight into how they are feeling.

1. Become fluent both verbally and non-verbally

Being able to hold a balanced conversation requires 2 things: knowing when to speak and when to be quiet. If you have a friend or colleague who dominates the conversation without pausing for breath, this is a monologue, not a conversation. Do you do this? Next time, think about how much space you take in the conversation, what tone you use, your choice of words and how you come across. Do you come across as too opinionated, indecisive or patronising?

2. Respect social rules and roles

Allowing for differences in social rules and roles in a diverse setting is a fundamental skill if you want to engage in a fully communicative exchange. Exhibiting rudeness, prejudices and insensitivity will not make you any friends. By being aware of the differences in social groups, ages, ethnicities, religions or cultural identities, you gain a much greater understanding of how someone is feeling. Be respectful of differences and receive respect in return.

3. Listening skills

Listening is crucial if you wish to understand the emotions of others. Instead of just waiting for your turn to speak, be fully engaged in what the other person is saying and pause to think about how they are feeling before you respond. Reiterate what they have said to show that you are with them and give them the time and the space to express themselves freely. Also note what they do not say and consider that not everyone finds it easy to open up completely.

4. Think about what triggers emotions

Put yourself in the other person's shoes and think about how you would feel if you had experienced something similar. This is the first step to empathy, which is a powerful tool in helping you to understand others. Remember though that I am not talking about sympathy, which has little constructive value and is not empowering. Saying, "It must have been a terrible experience," is a much more constructive response than, "I know exactly how you feel".

5. Be curious

Ask questions and show interest in the other person. Be aware of how they react physically when talking and note if they seem to feel uncomfortable or find it difficult to express themselves. Gentle coaxing is much more effective than being hostile or demanding explanations, so don't fall into that trap. Saying things like, "Spit it out", are not conducive to open communication but by asking tactful questions you can learn a lot that you didn't know.

Changing emotions in others

How can you change how someone else feels? Quite easily: the more positive you are, the more likely that positivity is to rub off on others. Being aware of your self-image and how you come across is vital if you want to lead a team, be a sports coach, raise emotionally healthy children or inspire others.

If your lecturer storms into the classroom with a stony face and is abrupt and condescending, you are soon going to lose interest in that lesson. When your boss skulks around the office looking like he is ready to blast anyone in his way, there will not be an atmosphere of productivity amongst your colleagues. As a parent, if you are continuously criticizing your kids, they are not going to look up to you as a positive role model.

But by doing the reverse, people's feelings and behavior can change. The lecturer who comes in with a smile and asks about the students with authentic kindness and concern will make you feel that he has your best interests at heart. The boss who spends time listening to your complaints and praises you regularly is more likely to nurture a loyal and productive team. The parent who allows for children to grow and make mistakes without criticism while supporting them at every step is raising loving, caring adults.

In a recent study carried out at Stanford University, psychologists looked at why people respond differently to similar situations and found that a lot of it is to do with how they 'want' to feel.

If you want to stay calm, you will most likely be able to do so even if faced by a very angry person. But if you want to feel angry, then you will be highly influenced by angry people and become angry yourself. The study reveals that we do have control over our emotions yet can be influenced by others, which means that we don't need to be affected so easily by negative or toxic vibes.

We can choose how we want to feel, but we can also influence others if they are open and desire to absorb our positive energy. The next time you make a tweet and receive friendly feedback, you are creating a safe space that encourages others to feel good about their opinions. If you make an angry rant about something that has been bothering you, you will receive an angry rant back from other users, and it can easily escalate into a case of mob rule.

Be mindful of how you portray yourself and the effect that it can have on others. Some people may choose to be miserable, but trying to change their mind is never a waste of time.

#5 Managing anxiety effectively

Anxiety is our body's natural response to stress.

Once you realize that, you are on the way to overcoming it. You may suffer from mild anxiety, which doesn't seem to have any obvious physical signs, but is a constant feeling that you just can't shake off. Whether you suffer from mild anxiety that makes your life more stressful or debilitating anxiety that needs immediate medical intervention, it is something that you can learn to control once you have recognized the triggers.

If you suffer from an anxiety disorder, this means that your emotions and behavior are altered, alongside experiencing physical symptoms. You may feel nervous, fearful, apprehensive and worried and this condition can lead to more serious episodes such as panic attacks and depression.

Ask yourself these two things:
• Do you have constant worries that you can generally ignore?

- Do you sometimes feel nervous, nauseated, shaky, or sweaty, but are not debilitated by these symptoms?

If your answer to both is yes, then you probably have some kind of mild anxiety which you manage to keep under control and it rarely becomes overwhelming. You can counteract those feelings by exercising regularly, which releases endorphins that calm your body and uses up adrenaline that is related to stress. A healthy diet can also help, as well as getting enough sleep and even learning relaxation and breathing techniques.

When you feel your heart beating faster in response to a stressful situation or your palms get sweaty and you have difficulty in breathing, then we are talking about more severe anxiety attacks, which can be very scary. Recognizing your triggers is extremely important and it could be anything from your commute to work or having to take an important exam. We all have different triggers, so developing self-awareness is crucial if you want to overcome severe anxiety.

A good practise to incorporate into your life is learning how to control your breathing. There is infinite evidence to show that as we do so, we can relieve ourselves of stress, tension and anxiety. Also, being able to sense the tension in your body and release it is a wonderful way to de-stress and useful in avoiding symptoms such as neck pain, headaches, dizziness and even long-lasting medical conditions like digestive problems. The health benefits of meditation and deep breathing are gaining ground and being incorporated into many therapies by trained professionals to overcome both mild and severe anxiety.

How can you help yourself? Begin by:

Identifying your thought patterns
What is going on in your mind as you begin to feel anxious? Is your sense of fear rational? Let's say you are waiting for your dental appointment and feel more and more anxious as time goes by. Stop and think! Your instinctive fear is not needed here – you aren't in any danger and the benefits of caring for your dental hygiene far outweigh the amount of stress that you are feeling. The more you fixate on your fear, the more your anxiety will grow. Tell yourself, "I will be OK" on repeat. Also, inform your dentist of your anxiety and trust him or her to be sensitive to your fears.

Overcoming fear of anxiety
Is the fear of anxiety causing you to be even more anxious? Sometimes, just

knowing that we are likely to feel anxious about a particular situation makes us even worse. Here's a tip – don't listen to that voice in your head telling you to worry. Your fear may be forcing you to avoid certain situations or people, such as accepting party invitations or a game of soccer, which is impoverishing your life and depriving you of the chance to have fun. Try going outside of your comfort zone now and again and learn to tolerate those feelings of nausea or nervousness, which will eventually fade. Don't be controlled by your fears.

How to stop being hard on yourself

If there is one thing that is essential if you want to overcome your bouts of anxiety, it is this: learn to be kinder to yourself. You are unique and special, and deserve to feel good about yourself, just like everyone else. This may be one of the hardest things I will be asking you to do, but believe me, once you begin to be kinder to yourself, you will be able to get rid of all of that anxiety.

As of tomorrow, I want you to to do at least 5 of these things every day:

1. Start each day by telling yourself that you are amazing and deserve to be happy
2. Don't believe everything you think. Create a new, more compassionate dialogue with yourself
3. Surround yourself with people who love you and have your back.
4. Stop comparing yourself to others. The only person you should compare yourself to is you.
5. End all toxic relationships. Don't let anyone who puts you down be a part of your life.
6. Pat yourself on the back and be proud of what you have achieved, no matter how small.
7. Embrace your individuality by wearing something special that reflects your personality.
8. Take time out each day to calm your mind. Concentrate on your breathing for a few minutes and clear your mind of any thoughts
9. Allow yourself to enjoy your passions and spend less time doing chores or trying to fulfill other people's expectations.
10. Carry out one small act of kindness each day for someone else, which will add to your sense of value and worth.
11. Give thanks each day for something good in your life and shift your energy to positive thoughts.
12. Forgive yourself. You may have messed up in the past on one or more occasions, but it's time to let that go. Use your mistakes to learn, mature

and grow.

The tide will turn

That bad place you are in won't last forever, even though it may not seem that way. Make plans for something that you want to do in the future and take small steps towards achieving that. If you dwell on the past, it is going to weigh down your present and prevent you from realizing a rewarding future. Things will get better, and you have to believe in that because the alternative is to remain stagnant and fearful of the future..

Breaking away from negative thought patterns

Focus on the positive aspects of your life and if you are finding that hard to do, think about why you are torturing yourself with negativity. What is the benefit of that? Write down on a piece of paper what is troubling you and then throw that paper in the waste bin. Dedicate your free time to doing something creative and express whatever you like through painting, gardening or whatever takes you away from thinking. Switch off, relax and focus on your dreams rather than your nightmares as you enjoy the feeling of contentment.

Dealing with panic attacks

If you suffer from panic attacks, you will know how distressing and also dangerous they can be. It is important to recognize that you are having a panic attack and to tell yourself that it is something temporary. Focus on your breathing by taking in deep breaths and counting to four before you exhale for four more seconds. This will reduce the hyperventilating, which is causing carbon dioxide to rise in your bloodstream. Concentrate on familiar physical sensations, like feeling the texture of your jeans, which will ground you in reality and alleviate your fears. Always carry a paper bag around with you, which you can blow into to help you readjust the oxygen levels in your body.

Often, the feeling of dread that you experience in a state of anxiety can have real physical manifestations that you need to be aware of. Mindfulness is a way to be present and to observe your emotions and sensations without loading yourself with guilt, shame or remorse. As you learn to practise emotional intelligence, you can handle yourself with greater ease and reduce stress in your life.

#6 Conquering low self-esteem

How low is your self-esteem?

Which of the following would you say describes how you feel about yourself:

- Lack of self-confidence
- Seeing yourself as unworthy
- Feeling inadequate
- Being incompetent
- Unlovable

Do you have any more negative feelings to add to the list? Being so critical of yourself is a surefire way to lower your self-esteem, which can have dire effects on your behavior, choices and relationships. Not only that, if you suffer from low self-esteem, you are more likely to develop mental health issues, depression and eating disorders, so you need to deal with it as soon as possible.

The term self-esteem means how a person feels about themselves. It is their belief they have abilities to do things and add value to others' lives. Those with a high level of self-esteem have been seen to be more successful and enjoy greater contentment in their lives. On the other hand, if you have low self-esteem, you are more likely to find it difficult to achieve your goals or build fruitful relationships.

The truth is that no one wants to feel that way, but low self-esteem usually begins in childhood and can be a hard habit to break. It becomes a pattern if you like; a way of looking at yourself and defining who you are. This is why you need to completely un-learn the way that you think about yourself and how you behave, which may seem challenging, but it's not impossible.

We talked a lot in Part Two about low self-esteem and its implications, so now it's time to turn things around and shake off those bad habits of putting yourself down. There is no miracle cure here, but if you can begin to reconnect with all of those negative feelings that you have about yourself and see that they don't represent you now, you can begin to regain a stronger sense of self.

And it goes without saying that wealth or material possessions don't protect you from low self-esteem – we already know that money can't buy happiness. Having a big job and a big bank balance are not going to make you feel any better if you feel inadequate inside. Those who seem to 'have it all' aren't necessarily living in a state of inner bliss and may even feel worthless and insecure.

Also, low self-esteem isn't something that you can just snap out of, like stopping biting your nails. There are a lot more complicated factors involved which have built up over time that are not only habit-forming but can distort your view of reality. Assuming that nothing will ever go your way means you won't bother trying for that new job and will shoot yourself in the foot to prove it. After all, you didn't deserve that new job anyway, right? Realising that the negative impact of your low self-esteem can seriously prevent you from moving on in life is the first step to taking control and strengthening your belief in yourself.

Combating self-criticism & accepting yourself

This is a two-step process that involves accepting who you are, with all your flaws, and realizing that no one is perfect, not even those influencers on Instagram. Self-criticism can be comparative (she's better than me) or internalized (I'm useless) and is your harsh, judgemental self talking to you.

Step 1.
You are buying into your own negative self-branding and hurting yourself in the process. So how do you get out of this vicious cycle?

- Be aware of the inclination to critique yourself and become an observer of those negative thoughts and complaints. Listen to what you are saying and remove yourself from this criticism.
- Be more honest with yourself. Sure you have flaws, but you also have strengths and that is what you need to focus on. Spend time with loved ones and engage them in conversation about your good points.
- Focus on your pride in your work rather than waiting for praise from others. Compliments may be nice, but they aren't always a true depiction of the value of your creativity. Be your own judge of whether or not you did a good job and don't rely on someone else's opinion, which may simply be lip-service.
- Follow your interests. Whatever you would like to do, be it learning how to ski or going to the cinema more often, take action by signing up for lessons or arranging a date with friends. You can even do both activities alone, and enjoy the sense of independence.

- Learn to love yourself. Every day is a new opportunity to recreate your life, so seize it. Make a personal mantra that you will repeat to yourself each morning on waking up, such as, "I am beautiful", or "I am clever". Be kinder to yourself and enjoy small pleasures with people who are important to you.
- Reflect on your mistakes and think about what you can do better next time. Make plans for the future and stop living in the past.

Step 2.

Comparing yourself constantly to others can lead to a deeper lack of self-esteem. If you are already down on yourself, it doesn't matter who you compare yourself to, they are always going to seem better than you. This has to stop.

- Be aware of your triggers and learn to avoid them. Social media is one of the first things that you should avoid as much as possible so reduce the time you spend scrolling and if possible, delete your accounts altogether.
- Don't spend time with people who have over-inflated egos because you will never be able to match up to their delusions of grandeur.
- Don't engage in conversation with those who you feel are prying into your life and eager to put you down. Hang out with friends and family who have your back instead.
- Be conscious of envy when it arises, and recognize that it is a very toxic emotion that will not bring you happiness. There is always someone in a worse position than you, so stay with that thought instead.

Dealing with doubt, fear, and uncertainties of change

Your self-doubt and fear of change or uncertainties will keep you trapped in a life that you don't enjoy. Is that really what you want? I am sure that your answer will be no, hopefully!

You may have big goals but feel that you can't accomplish them because that little voice in your head is telling you that you can't do it. It is keeping you stuck in a rut and preventing you from moving forward, feeding on your insecurities and fears. It may be too late for you now to be a World Champion in kick-boxing or pursue a career in medicine, but that doesn't stop you from having goals that are attainable. You just need to believe in yourself and make the first move.

Any change in life is scary, whether that is moving house or deciding to have children, and that uncertainty about the future can be a barrier to your emotional growth and future happiness. Once you accept that change is an inevitable part of life, you are ready to make it happen.

1. Make a note of what you are uncertain about and then write down what roadblocks may exist along the way. Once you take the fear out of the unknown, you will be able to move ahead.
2. Knock down your psychological walls and look at what is making you doubt yourself. Does it make sense to be uncertain about each of these things? Examine the evidence for and against and reassess your assumptions about reality.
3. Recall any prior accomplishments to strengthen your self-confidence. Remember that award you won at school or the job you nailed, even when you thought you weren't good enough? Keep those achievements in mind whenever you feel self-doubt creeping in.
4. Assess what is needed for you to achieve your goals. Write down what is required to secure them and work on acquiring any missing skills, information or courses that will equip you better.
5. Create a plan of action and use it as an outline to steer you forward. Prepare yourself for the obstacles you may encounter along the way and also be prepared to encounter failure. If you focus on minimizing risks, you will be better equipped for anything and can even turn obstacles into opportunities.

What not to do

Sometimes, it's difficult to escape the pattern of being down on yourself; after all, you are used to it. You get into certain thought cycles and habits that keep you enslaved in a negative self-image of who you are and what you are capable of. I want you to try to make the effort to avoid making the same mistakes by applying the following 'don'ts:

1. Don't put other people's needs and wants before your own. This won't earn you any respect.
2. Don't keep apologizing for things that aren't your fault just to appease someone. You do not need to apologize for things that are out of your control.
3. Don't go along with others just because you don't want to 'rock the boat'. State assertively your desires and preferences, no matter what.
4. Don't undervalue your worth, whether that be in a job or a relationship. Maintain your standards and stand by your value as a partner or employee.
5. Don't keep changing your mind to fit in with someone else. Stand up

for your beliefs and be ready to justify them if needs be.

6. Don't let others encroach on your boundaries. Clearly express how you feel when someone oversteps the mark.

7. Don't try to ingratiate yourself with people by buying excessive gifts or over-flattering them – it isn't necessary in order to feel appreciated.

8. Don't dwell on whether someone will like you or not. You can't control how other people will react or what perceptions they have.

9. Don't talk yourself down and engage in a negative self-dialogue. It is destructive and not going to make you feel good about yourself.

10. Don't try to be perfect – no one is!

How to stop overthinking

Overthinking can be exhausting.

Thinking of a few things at a time is OK, but when it becomes chronic, it is counterproductive and increases pressure on ourselves. Deliberating endlessly over how to make a decision about something that is relatively straightforward and then questioning the final decision or trying to predict the outcome of the decision over and over again can wear you down.

This rumination can disturb your sleep, affect your eating patterns and seriously damage your relationships with others, who will feel frustrated and tired. Worrying about ifs and buts and going over why this or that happened is a complete waste of your mental energy and you are not likely to ever find the answers. Getting out of this loop can be extremely difficult and not coming to any conclusions can cause more anxiety and stress.

You may be fearful of the future or feel insecure about it and so you are trying to solve the problems in your head when in actual fact, that is probably impossible to do as we cannot always predict the future.

Here's how to defeat that pattern of overthinking and get your life back:

1. As soon as a thought pops into your head, replace it with a different one. One way to do this is to prepare a list of 'other' thoughts, such as your favorite movies or food. Use them as gap fillers instead of obsessing about a particular thought.

2. Cultivate a little bit of psychological distance from your present situation. Instead of worrying about what could go wrong, think of the advantages when all goes well.

3. Rephrase the conversation. Instead of saying to yourself, "I'm not happy in my job", talk to yourself about what job would make you feel more fulfilled, and think of what you need to do to achieve that.

4. Write down everything that is playing on your mind before you go to bed each night. This way, you get them out of your system and will feel relieved of the pressure to come up with answers.

5. Pay more attention to your senses and focus on sounds, smells and tastes, Reconnect with the sensory side of yourself and give your brain a well-earned rest.

6. Engage in physical exercise, which will make you focus more on your body and less on your thoughts.

7. Recognize that your brain is overworked and give it a break. Do something that amuses you or something that you find relaxing, and enjoy the sensation of not having to think.

8. Practise mindfulness, which is not about your mind, but about simply observing the state you are in. Allow yourself to focus only on your breathing and don't let your thoughts interfere with that.

Learn to not get lost in your thoughts of what could have been or what didn't happen. It is useless and not relevant to your present. Mental stress can seriously impact your quality of life and an over-active mind will leave you feeling unable to cope. With practice, you can train your brain to perceive things differently and allow yourself peace.

#7 Overcoming disappointment

Are you feeling disappointed with your life?

Or maybe you are disappointed with a loved one, or even with yourself. Well, we can't always get what we want and life is unpredictable, so when things don't go right for us, we are left feeling frustrated, disillusioned, angry and disappointed. It's like someone or something deliberately wants to stop us from feeling good when everything was going so well. If you continuously get one disappointment after another, that can drag you down and make you feel miserable.

It could be something trivial, like going to the local store and discovering it is closed or watching a highly-acclaimed movie only to end up not liking it. Most disappointments of that nature don't disturb our daily life that much and we can deal with them. They aren't that important and we can shrug them off quite easily.

More serious disappointment may come when we bank on something or take a risk, such as applying for a new job or buying a new home – the time and in many cases money that we have invested seem to be equal to the expectation we have that everything will work out. Not getting the job may be a setback and finding that your new home has severe rising damp is a bummer, but both are fixable.

Maybe the worst type of disappointment is the emotional kind when you feel let down by someone that you cared about or trusted – that's a crushing blow which is hard to overcome as you are swamped with feelings of blame, resentment and even rage. Questions such as, "How could they do that to me?" come to mind and you may even begin to feel that you did something wrong to cause the situation.

It seems that the more emotionally invested in someone or something, the greater the disappointment we feel when things go wrong. Think of the last time you felt seriously disappointed, and it is probably in relation to how someone treated you. It may have been a matter of faith, trust, belief or love so your emotions will definitely have been affected.

This kind of disappointment is the result of the expectations that we set for others. It's not some universal truth or paradigm of reality but is based on our own standards and values. Disappointment comes when we have expectations, and it's these expectations which can lead to disappointment. You expect your partner to love you, right? You expect your friends to honor the trust that you put in them, right? You expect your family to have your back, right?

So when your partner tells you he/she doesn't love you, your friend betrays you and your family turn their back on you in time of need, you will naturally feel deeply disappointed. The idea that you cannot get what you want is a crushing blow that most people can cope with, while others find it difficult to bounce back from. If you suffer from low self-esteem or lack of motivation, disappointment can be a decisive factor in your overall wellness as well as your future relationships and ambitions.

The realization that you didn't get what you wanted can make you feel angry, which will keep you ignited until it gives way to sadness and even apathy. The stress-induced by your feeling of losing something that you thought you had in the bag can lead to aggression, guilt and eventually depression. Add to that a sense of remorse, loneliness and worry as well as physiological symptoms like headaches, hot and cold flashes, nausea, tingling sensations and tiredness.

Basically, your brain goes from a state of euphoria to hopelessness, just like that. If you are an avid fan of your local soccer team, you may go through some of these emotions when they lose in the league final. Once those feelings subside, you will probably continue to support them and look forward to next season in which you are sure they will do better. In a deeper emotional disappointment, this isn't so easy to do, although it is possible.

Disappointment stimulates the parasympathetic nervous system and brings on feelings of melancholy and inertia, which can lead to serious stress-induced conditions if not checked, such as heart disease, digestive disorders and depressed immune system. Now add to that feeling disappointed in yourself after something like a disagreement, criticism, insult or failing to achieve one of your goals.

No one can be more unkind to you than your own ego, which may have set the bar so high that any criticism or failure means that you impose a life sentence of misery on yourself. The more down you feel, the more difficult it will be to pull yourself up. But hope is not lost: with a little practise and some introspection, you can overcome those feelings of disappointment and learn to get back on track much easier. Here's how:

1. Rethink your expectations
You know that saying, 'don't build your hopes up', which is the same as saying not to have too high expectations, in order to avoid disappointment. This is a practical stance to take when things are not in your hands, such as the result of a soccer game or a competition that you have entered. By telling yourself that you didn't expect to win, you will lower the feeling of disappointment as you replace the original memory.

2. Learn to be emotionally self-sufficient
When you enter into a long-term relationship, the most common development is an emotional attachment to your partner and vice versa. It's easy to make too many compromises and to gradually lose your individuality as you take on the role of being 'a couple'. If your relationship ends, as they often do, you will probably feel completely devastated, as if you have 'lost your other half'. Think about how much of your sense of self you gave up and go into your next relationship with a reserve of 'you', rather than just 'we'.

3. Reappraise what you want
Consider your strengths and weaknesses and make a checklist of what you would like to change or improve on. Don't set yourself impossible tasks,

but work with your strengths to plan new objectives that are doable. Focus on your weaknesses and look at ways of improving your skills, knowledge or expertise. By being proactive, you are investing in your future wellbeing.

4. Control your attachments

The more emotionally attached you are to something, the more let-down you will feel when something goes wrong. This isn't to say that you should be cold and uncaring, but try to invest in causes or activities in moderation, rather than becoming fanatical. You can still support your local team, but if their loss means that you are devastated, you need to find other ways to boost your spirits.

The main secret to overcoming disappointments is to improve the minor ones. The more disappointments we notch up, the more cortisol and adrenaline are stimulated by the brain. Eventually, every minor setback feels like a massive blow, making us overreact and feel worse than we did before.

5. Change your perspective

Here are some examples of how to change the way you deal with minor disappointments:

- *Improve*: Sure, you are disappointed, but think about what you can do to improve for next time.
- *Failure*: Learn what to do to succeed
- *Disagreement*: You may not be right, but at least you maintain your respect and feeling of self-worth.
- *Criticism*: Focus on what is true and work on improving.
- *Insults*: Recognize your value and don't let words get to you.
- *Loss of affection*: Continue to share compassion, affection and kindness.
- *Loss of love*: Grieve and then continue to self-love and to feel worthy of love
- *Loss of trust*: Continue to believe in yourself, your values and your humanity.

Finally, try to see disappointments as speed bumps — they are meant to make you slow down, but not to stop you from moving forward. Disappointments are a part of life and are thrown at us without warning, but you can be prepared by building up your self-esteem, removing the fear of failure and being in touch with your emotions, all of which we have covered in the previous sections.

#8 Forging better relationships

How connected are you?

How many good friends do you have that you hang out with regularly, and how close are you to your family members or partner?

We all have relationships, and couldn't do without them as social beings. Social development is an integral part of our emotional and physiological development and most of us feel happier and healthier when we are involved in meaningful relationships. Elderly people especially show lower levels of diabetes, arthritis, hypertension and emphysema when they feel a sense of belonging.

Unless you chose to live the solitary life of a hermit in a far-away wilderness or desert island, you will most likely want and need to have strong ties in your life. You may have childhood friends that you still keep in touch with or have been in a long-term relationship with a partner for many years. Also, of course, you could have parents, siblings, children and other extended family members. Often, we are so caught up in our day job that we have little time to spend with the people that mean the most to us in our lives. This can cause a strain on the ties that bind and also have an adverse effect on how we feel about ourselves

If you have ever moved to a new town, job or joined a new gym, you will know that feeling of discomfort at not having any friends/family nearby or not knowing anyone. Usually, it doesn't take much time before you are chatting with your new neighbors or colleagues and meeting for coffee with new-found friends. It may be great to experience solitude to nurture your creativity or find some peace, but we also need to nurture deep, meaningful relationships for our physical and mental wellbeing.

Today, more than ever, we also have the option of connecting 'virtually' with others; people who we may never meet in 'real' life. While some may frown on such relationships as 'not valid', I have personally built up many friendships with people who share similar interests to me over the years on various social media platforms. The use of webcams and Zoom-like apps means that it is easy to chat to someone face to face who may be halfway across the world and even though you may never actually meet that person, you can add them to your Rolodex of 'friends' if you feel like it.

Having said that, it is useful to have the discretion to be able to distinguish between those who you have a healthy online connection with and those who are just a name on your Facebook, Twitter or Snapchat account. At the same time, you may have 'acquaintances' who you bump into at the local pool or yoga class that you don't have any special bond with and with whom you probably won't develop an intimate relationship with in the future.

All relationships need nurturing, otherwise, they can deteriorate over time. People who have a high level of emotional intelligence tend to be better than those with low emotional intelligence at maintaining such healthy ties. As you read earlier, the ability to recognize your emotions and control them, as well as being able to understand the emotions of others, brings more success in relationships. Having greater self-awareness helps you to handle emotions in a way that enhances your connection with others.

If you can acquire more emotional intelligence, you are more equipped to recognize when your friend or partner is hurt, disappointed, sad or feeling down and you will be less likely to respond in an angry or confrontational manner. You will also be able to tell the difference in the nuances of that person's behavior and have more insight into what is going on with them. This gives you the tools you need to make more informed decisions, handle conflict better and create deeper bonds.

Here are some hacks for you to be more aware of your reactions and to nurture more fulfilling relationships and create stronger ties in the form of questions that I want you to ask yourself. Consider your answers to each one and think about what you can do to improve your relationships with your nearest and dearest.

1. When your partner complains that you are always grumpy, ask yourself:
• Am I able to identify with how he/she feels?
• Am I quick to react without thinking or understanding the complaint?
• Can I be less reactive and more proactive?
• Can I bring calmness to the situation?
• Can I express my emotions?

2. Your colleague criticizes you for taking too long to complete a task:
• Can you remain calm during the disagreement?
• Can you understand why he/she is upset?
• Can you prevent the conflict from escalating?
• Can you handle the criticism without letting your emotions get the better

of you?

• Can you find a way to rectify the situation?

Dealing with romantic relationships

Ah, love! That elusive emotion which, when captured, can quickly turn to hate. Romantic relationships and break-ups must account for 90% of misery in the world. That might be a slight exaggeration, but I am sure that there have been times in your life when you have felt 'in love', 'deliriously happy' only then to be followed by being 'totally heartbroken'.

But in all seriousness, maintaining a deep and meaningful romantic relationship can be hard work, once all of the initial fireworks have gone out and you slip into 'couple' mode. Maintaining a healthy intimate partnership takes dedication and a lot of hard work, which we are not always aware of or willing to do. Often, we are unable to because of past issues, events or fears, which hold us back from committing 100%. Have you ever wondered how some marriages or partnerships seem to thrive and survive for years while others quickly fizzle out? Couples who exhibit emotional intelligence seem to be good at strengthening and developing their relationship as time goes by because they have the ability to be aware of, control and express emotions in a healthy manner.

Having strong communication skills is also a very important aspect. It's all about being in touch with your feelings and understanding your partner's too. Empathy comes into its own when we talk about any kind of relationship, but especially with a life partner. Having the patience to listen, the desire to understand and the willingness to express in a loving way are all part of emotional intelligence.

Once you have established trust and commitment, there are other points that you can focus on, all of which require you to use your emotional intelligence to maintain a loving relationship:

1. Be friends
A friend is someone who you support and care about and should also apply to your partner. Being friends means that you share time with each other, understand one another and enjoy the company and companionship that your relationship brings. When you see your partner as a friend, they may remain a friend for life!

2. Have respect

Having respect and deep admiration for your partner is essential. If you do not honor their needs and wishes, it will not last, and if it does, there will be a striking imbalance. If you appreciate your partner's qualities, achievements and abilities, demonstrate that often, and you will also earn their respect.

3. Communicate

When communication breaks down between a couple, the relationship needs fixing, otherwise, it will not be able to function. When you acquire emotional intelligence, you are better equipped to

convey your thoughts, feelings and needs in a healthy manner. A dysfunctional relationship will lack this open communication, either from one or both sides, and will prevent the relationship from flourishing.

4. Manage conflict

Use emotional intelligence to navigate conflict and disagreements. You don't have to agree on everything, but if you can listen, understand the other perspective and respect it, conflict will be greatly reduced. Being able to exercise compromise can also play a crucial part in binding you together and give each side space to maintain their beliefs without feeling that they are committing an act of betrayal.

5. Nurture your relationship

Emotionally intelligent couples nurture the relationship by appreciating the value of each other as an individual as well as a couple. Encouraging your partner to pursue his or her passions instead of feeling insecure will strengthen the bond that you have, rather than fill you with the fear that you are 'losing' your partner.

6. Maintain healthy boundaries

Create space for your partner to be themselves and allow a platform for honesty at all times. If you have an open arena for discussion, each will be clearer of where they stand in the relationship and yet feel more secure. Creating restrictive boundaries and feelings of frustration can have disastrous effects.

7. Share a meaningful life

Emotionally intelligent couples are aware of what is meaningful to each other and want to share that together. Find ways to connect on a regular basis and enjoy a few shared activities, even if it is something as simple as clearing the dining table together. Be mindful of the importance of practising love in every area of your relationship.

Remember that when it comes to relationships, you can set the goalposts by being aware of your own emotions and acknowledging theirs. Compassion, respect, empathy and communication are all essential elements that you can use every day to form stronger, happier bonds.

#9 Working towards a healthy body

How good do you feel about yourself?

Do you maintain a regular exercise program or are you a couch potato? Do you have a positive body image or are you already thinking about your next plastic surgery? There can be no doubt that our relationship with our body can be complicated and feeling happy with your appearance of fitness level also means that you feel happier in general.

But how we look is only part of the story. No one is going to argue against keeping fit and taking pride in one's appearance; it also boosts our self-esteem when we feel at our best physically, but being overweight or comparing ourselves continually to others can lower our 'feel good' vibes. Body image is indeed a source of stress for many, especially women, although practising self-compassion and self-worth can overcome those negative emotions.

When we change our perceptions about how we look, that can have a positive impact on how we think of ourselves. Self-image is exactly that – how we think of ourselves – and is something that builds up over time. If you have allowed yourself to have a negative perception of your self-image, that is what you will see when you look in the mirror, which is also directly linked to your feelings of self-esteem.

Do you have a positive or negative self-image? Take a look at the following statements and select the ones that apply to you:

• Do you see yourself as attractive and desirable?
• Do you see yourself as smart and intelligent?
• Do you see a happy, healthy person when you look in the mirror?
• Do you believe that you are close to being your ideal version of yourself?
• Do you think that others perceive you as all of the above?

If you answered yes to most of these questions, that's great! If you have a few 'nos' in there, then you need to look more closely at what is going on to make you react negatively. Here are some pointers to help you:

1. List 10 things you love about yourself
2. List 10 skills you possess
3. List 10 things you appreciate about your life
4. List 5 achievements you are proud of
5. List 5 occasions where you overcame a challenge

Once you remove the 'negatives' and focus on the 'positives', you gain a better perspective not only of yourself, but of life in general. Taking care of your body is an important strategy to fight disease and delay health problems associated with aging, such as arthritis, dementia and general mobility. The truth is, if you feel good on the inside, it will show on the outside, and your health will thank you for it.

I hope that you feel better already about your self-image!

The mind-body connection

Is it all in your mind?

There can be no doubt that there is a direct relation between our body and mind. We have touched on the fact several times in this book when talking about how our emotional state can cause serious health issues. As we learn more about the power of the mind, traditional eastern ideas and techniques such as meditation and mindfulness have become fully integrated into therapies and treatments for a wide range of psychological disorders. Yoga is even taught in some kindergartens now and the whole wellness lifestyle has become part of the mainstream culture.

The mind-body connection can be observed particularly well in cases of trauma. Our brain has different mechanisms for dealing with threats, and neural regulators get to work in the brain cortex, the immune response and the hypothalamic-pituitary-adrenal, and gut-brain axes. When we face trauma, our cardiac regulation is aroused and the fight-flight response kicks in (which is the activation of the sympathetic nervous system). In the face of an unavoidable threat, the freeze response is stimulated and once the threat has gone, the parasympathetic system overrides, bringing what is called quiescent immobility.

If you undergo sustained periods of negative emotional states like stress, anxiety and depression, your immune system can suffer, which affects your bodily functions. On the other hand, when you experience positive emotions, studies have shown an improvement in reducing ill health, reducing pain and increasing longevity. There is even evidence to suggest that such positive emotions can enhance immunity in conditions such as cancer and HIV, as well as after exposure to the flu virus.

How can you improve your mind-body wellbeing?

Meditate

There is a massive amount of evidence now coming to light on how meditation can have truly healing benefits. If you are still a bit dubious about that, here's my suggestion: try it!

When a recent study was carried out to see the effects on the brain of meditation, it was observed that experienced meditators showed more brain activity in the region related to attention and inhibition response than novice meditators. Researchers also noticed less activity in areas of the brain concerned with discursive emotions and cognitions, which suggests a direct correlation to brain plasticity

Meditation doesn't have to take up too much of your time – just ten minutes a day is enough to get you into a calm and relaxed state. As you become accustomed to focussing on your inhalation and exhalation, you will notice that your body relaxes and your mind cuts out all of the noise around you. It is a simple way to regain a sense of balance and once you experience it, you will probably go on to become an expert! Those who incorporate some kind of meditation into their daily routine claim to have a great sense of inner peace, which is directly related to positivity.

Be mindful

Mindfulness meditation helps you to manifest emotional intelligence and to become more self-aware. It can improve your ability to comprehend your own emotions, help you learn how to recognize the emotions of others and strengthen your ability to control your emotions. Knowing how to use your emotions correctly is a valuable skill that can help you to approach a situation with the right mindset and to achieve your goals.

The next time you feel some kind of negativity creeping in, pause for a moment and tune in to that emotion, Observe it and acknowledge it for what it is. Stay with it for a moment and allow it to dissipate. Being aware, or mindful, of that emotion is the first step to mastering it and allowing you to handle your inner self.

Keeping fit

Being active and in a good physical condition is not only beneficial to our health. It also contributes to our sense of wellbeing and self-esteem. Often though, we don't have the discipline to maintain a regular exercise program and when we feel low, it doesn't come easy to most of us to get out and do a tiring work-out or a five-kilometer run.

Partaking in some kind of physical exercise can help us build up our resilience, which helps us to adapt and recover quickly from setbacks and meet challenges with greater ease, so it is definitely something that you should begin to incorporate into your life. Exercise also helps to improve our attention and manage our energy levels.

You can alleviate a lot of built-up tension and stress by working out, which is crucial if you wish to rid yourself of negativity and frustration. By disciplining the body, you are disciplining the mind, whether you do taekwondo or dance – both body and mind are working in unison. Your heart will certainly thank you for it, playing a large part in your ability to self-regulate through breathing techniques.

Nasal breathing patterns have a positive effect on our physiology and when done properly, take excessive pressure off our cardiovascular system with lower heart rates and increased heart rate variability. As we strengthen our respiratory system, we can control the length, depth and pace of our heart rate, giving us more power over our physical, mental and emotional selves.

Eating healthily

Not only can you improve your emotional intelligence by working through all of the above, but you can also apply your new-found skills to your eating habits. We all know that we are what we eat, but how we eat can play a large role in helping us gain control of our lives and aid our digestion.

Preparing what you eat with care, savoring each bite and being mindful of the whole experience without over-eating or rushing your meal can help you to enhance your emotional intelligence.

• Begin by being aware of your hunger and when you are full
• Ask yourself what and why you are eating
• Establish a regular eating routine and stick to it

- Apply impulse control around pleasurable food that may not be so good for you
- Prepare a relaxed setting for your meals
- Be mindful of what you eat when you feel emotional
- Don't snack whenever you feel like it
- Look for ways to eat a healthier diet
- Eat with friends more often

Our obsession with food in the west is very much oriented towards what's in the food rather than how to enjoy it. New food fads and diets are here one day and gone the next, as we focus more and more on what we eat and how much or little of it. Go to any Mediterranean country or traditional community in the East and you will discover that mealtime is not just about eating – it is an opportunity to gather with friends and family, to laugh, and to bond. The food may be tasty and is usually locally sourced according to what is seasonally available, but it is more about the ritual of being together and sharing. In addition, it's not unusual for a meal to last hours, with each bite being savored with good company. Why not add some of that to your life!

Cutting down on alcohol, etc.

Low self-esteem, anxiety, stress, trauma and depression have all been linked with unhealthy habits such as alcohol and drug abuse, as well as smoking. On the other hand, people with a high level of emotional intelligence tend to exhibit a healthier take on the subject and are less likely to engage in harmful indulgences.

If you are a heavy drinker, smoker or practise another kind of substance abuse and would like to stop, there are many organisations and professional therapists who can help you and support you through the process.

At the end of the day, it all comes down to the basic tenets of emotional intelligence. Once you begin to embrace them, you may find the courage that you need to begin living a healthier life.

Self-awareness

By knowing your strengths and weaknesses, you can eventually come to confront the problem and begin to identify triggers. This is not an easy task and will take time, support, patience and self-love.

Self-regulation

Now that you are aware of the problem and have identified your triggers, you can apply techniques such as delaying gratification or learning to relax more. When you begin to master ways to deal with stress and gain a higher level of self-esteem, you can work towards overcoming your habits.

Motivation

You will need to find the motivation to achieve your goals and the mental fortitude to keep at it. Focus on the positive aspects of your efforts and remember how far you have come. Discipline is paramount but only do as much as you can, one day at a time.

Compassion

Self-compassion is essential while beating yourself up will take you nowhere. Share your fears and doubts with your loved ones and use their support to reinforce your commitment. Also, have empathy for their situation to – they cannot help you otherwise and you may lose their valuable support.

Social skills

Build yourself a strong network of caring people and spend as much time with them as possible. Enjoy doing things together and take up invitations to hang out, go mountain trekking, or whatever will get you out of the house and away from your negative thoughts.

No one else is going to look after you, so it's up to you to make sure that you maintain good health, both mentally and physically. Strengthen your mind and your body, because the one relies on the other, and together they will carry you through all challenges in life.

#10 Patience and discipline

How much patience do you have?

You probably get frustrated when you have to wait in line at the bank or on finding out that the train will be 10 minutes late. Standing around when you have better things to do can be so frustrating. Listening to your friend whine on and on about problems at work can also wear your patience when you would rather talk about something else. Teaching your child to tie his or her shoelaces can drive you nuts, and you may as well end up doing it yourself, right?

We all seem to be in such a hurry to get from here to there or to move on to the next thing. It seems that we have forgotten that patience is actually classed as a virtue by many, alongside kindness, humility, honesty and so on. The truth is that we have no time to wait anymore and are used to having everything on demand. It wasn't so long ago that you had to wait about five minutes for your dial-up internet to connect, and that's a modest number. Today, if you aren't online within a split-second, panic sets in and your blood begins to boil as you yell. "I have no internet!"

As the pressure builds up, frustration and stress begin to take over. Your heart rate goes up, you become agitated and unable to control your emotions. At some point, such as when the elderly lady ahead of you at the cash desk is still fumbling around with her groceries, you may be tempted to make some exasperating statement or make a plain mean comment. Not a nice way to go about things.

But having patience can do you the world of good because you avoid working yourself up into a state of annoyance or upset. Think about it; being able to wait without becoming irate and agitated has to have its advantages. It does: when you acquire more patience, you deal with such delays in a much calmer manner so that your inner peace isn't disturbed. When you develop emotional intelligence and learn to control your emotions more effectively, waiting stops becoming a chequered flag for you to spiral into a rage.

Having the ability to master your feelings and impulses in a 'challenging' situation takes mental strength. It's much easier to huff and puff and go into a rant than to remain composed and calm. I'm not suggesting that you become indifferent or passive – no one wants to be kept hanging around – I'm asking you to consider the benefits to your wellbeing of accepting situations and having the clarity to control your thoughts and deeds. When you realize that not everything is within your control, you will alleviate yourself of the stress that impatience brings to your life.

That goes for things that you are looking forward to or working towards as well. Being excited at the prospect of going on your long-planned vacation is a positive feeling, and that type of anticipation is a healthy emotion to have. Feeling miserable because you still have a month to wait, is not. When that sense of impatience spurs you on to be more dynamic and determined, it is a great impulse that can help you achieve your future goals. It will fuel your actions and help you to focus on what you want to achieve. It's the negative kind of impatience that causes you to lose your self-control that you need to handle.

Think about the last time you 'lost your patience' and how you reacted. The term itself implies by definition that we are not in control of our feelings, as if patience is something autonomous that comes and goes as it pleases. You are actually making excuses for your bad behaviour and trying to justify it by blaming 'patience'; an independent entity with a life of its own!

It is much, much harder to master self-control than it is to be emotionally reactive, which is probably why we all blame someone or something else for our outbursts. It's the easy way out, isn't it? Impatience can become a habit and our default reaction to triggers from external and internal stimuli. When things don't go as we had planned or the way we want them to go, our thoughts send a signal to the brain that activates a certain emotional response, be that frustration, anxiety or anger.

When you have it together and are in control of your emotions, those triggers don't have any effect on you anymore and you remain calm, balanced and unaffected. This requires a certain amount of discipline but you don't have to be a Zen master to do that. You simply need to be more mindful of your thoughts, emotions and responses. Impatience is always about frustration and often the 'why me' dialogue begins when your flight is cancelled. In fact, you are relating your present predicament with past experiences too ("this always happens to me") and future expectations ("how long will I have to wait until I get what I want?").

Here's where you can practise mindfulness, which is the state of objective, non-judgemental and non-attached awareness. The flight cancellation didn't just happen to you – it also happened to another 340 people. Just because you have had flights cancelled in the past, doesn't mean it is a conspiracy against you personally. And not being able to get what you want, when you want it, is a fact of life. If you take time to examine your frustration at this present moment, you will see it for what it is – self-induced stress.

The benefits of patience

In case you are still not convinced, here are some benefits of mastering patience:

Better decision-making
Patience gives you the time to reassess the situation and to weigh up the pros and cons of your next decision, rather than acting on impulse. In the case of the cancelled flight, instead of working yourself up into a fluster, sit down and calmly work through alternatives. Accept that this is how things

stand and think about your next step.

Less stress and a healthier life

Instead of becoming overwhelmed by negative emotions such as anger and frustration, having patience allows you to process situations in a calmer context without raising your blood pressure. It is said that we lose 10 minutes of our life for every one minute of anger, and those who lead long, happy lives seem to have learnt to master patience very successfully.

More understanding and empathy

Take time to process what you are enduring and think of others in the same boat as you. How do they feel and what negative emotions are they experiencing which may be based on a much more serious urgency than your own? Your impatience to get to work in a hurry although stuck in traffic can easily be countered by someone being rushed to the hospital in an ambulance for emergency care, right?

Insight into the process of personal growth

Monitoring your emotional responses to situations might not seem that important now, but as you continue to do so, you will learn to grow and become clearer about your abilities and potential. Learning to be patient without overreacting can serve you well in future scenarios where calm objectivity is essential, such as in a work meeting or during a family crisis.

Impatience is a kind of self-induced chaos as we try relentlessly to swim against the tide. When you fret about controlling things that clearly aren't in your domain, you are filling yourself with frustration and disappointment. The more effort you put into trying to relax, the calmer you will feel. There are some other bonuses to patience, which include the following:

- Peacefulness on a daily basis
- Greater clarity, focus and perspective
- Being a better listener
- Being nicer to others
- Being kinder and more caring

Self-discipline is not an easy habit to adopt. You are probably OK at behaving in line with rules and regulations imposed by others, but may not be so good at keeping your emotions in line. As a kid, you may have been punished for behaving badly and rewarded when you were good. This is a normal parenting technique used by many, although it is not necessarily the best way to teach children self-discipline. It may have a negative impact on their emotional development and sense of responsibility.

If kids only behave well for fear of being caught out, then what does that say about us as adults? If your only incentive for obeying the law is the fear of being arrested and convicted of a crime, how does that correlate with your sense of morality? And if you only behave well in order to receive some kind of external reward, how does that reflect on your sense of self-worth and value?

If we grow up with the idea that our actions have consequences, good or bad, then we learn to act without focussing on our inner sense of balance and self-regulation. If we are called out for being rude to a colleague, we assume that we deserve the criticism. If we help an old lady across the road, we expect a thank you. Learning to be motivated by our true, authentic self, requires discipline.

If you want to set the example, be an inspiration to others and build deeper connections with people, emotional discipline is the missing key. I'm talking here about controlling how you behave and feel, not to score any points, but because you want to take ownership of your inner happiness. When you practice emotional discipline, you don't always do what you want to do or say what you want to say. You avoid acting on impulse and expressing anger or frustration just because you feel like it.

A lack of self-discipline can lead to your behavior coming across as offensive, hostile and upsetting to others. As well as that, it may incorrectly portray who you are and create a false impression.

- Saying exactly what is on your mind doesn't show consideration for how others will receive it.
- Avoiding conversations which may make you fall out of favor with someone will not resolve conflicts or build stronger bonds.
- Holding back your opinion or belief or being passive will not earn you respect.
- Taking sides just to feel part of the pack may betray your true values and beliefs

The above examples will not earn you trust, respect or admiration, as people are very capable of seeing through inauthentic and ingratiating behavior. Emotional discipline involves recognizing how to handle your emotions in different circumstances, such as when you receive criticism.

Responding in anger or becoming defensive is not the way to go about it. Rather, knowing how to react appropriately by controlling what you say and do will produce a much better outcome.

Here are some tips to help you gain more control over your emotions and to self-regulate your inner responses and outward behavior:

What's the cause?

Try to identify what triggers that emotion of frustration or anger. Is the comment by your partner about your weight hitting a nerve? Does it have to do with your low self-esteem and your self-image?

Do a body scan

When you do a body scan, you can detect the location of that physical reaction to your emotions. Are you clenching your jaw or feel a thumping headache coming on? Locate that physical sensation of anger and grade it in intensity from 1 to 5. Now try to relax the muscles in that area and feel the relief.

What's on your mind?

What thoughts are coming into your mind as you experience those negative emotions? Are your thoughts fuelling them? If you are thinking, "no one should talk to me like that", is it making you calmer or angrier?

Expose your weaknesses

Which part of yourself is this emotion covering for? Is it your fear of rejection or your insecurity about your abilities? Focus on whatever you sense is the real issue and put the emotion to one side.

These are very simple steps that you can take in any situation and you can even do them now when you are in a calm state. Practise the art of self-discipline whenever you can so that you will be more prepared when impatience, frustration, anger and chaos threaten your inner well-being.

Delaying gratification

You've probably seen the cute TikTok video of toddlers being asked by their parents to resist eating the treats placed in front of them until mum or dad re-enters the room a few minutes later. Most of the kids do surprisingly well in resisting the temptation to eat the caramels because the praise that they expect to receive from their parents for accomplishing the task greatly outweighs the instant gratification of gobbling everything up there and then.

That's an interesting observation and although some children do succumb to a quick nibble (who wouldn't), they deny having done so to their parents because they don't want to lose that hug and words of praise. This kind of behavior is essential to self-regulation and self-control.

A similar 'experiment' carried out in 1972 known as the 'Marshmallow Test' showed that children who were best able to wait grew up into young adults more socially and academically successful at high-school. Another study showed that high-school students who could wait a week for a monetary reward were more likely to get higher grades, show less behavioral problems in school and be less likely to use drugs, alcohol and cigarettes than those who chose not to wait.

Despite the research, we live in a world of quick-fixes and band-aid solutions, with instantaneous gratification at the swipe of our cell phone or the touch of a button. What's the point in exercising patience or delaying pleasure when we can have it all now? Where is the value in having patience or working towards a future goal when we can enjoy today? Wouldn't you rather spend all of your disposable income at fancy restaurants than saving up for a retirement plan, which is only going to be useful years from now?

You may be right, but imagine yourself in 10, 20 or 30 years from now living a meagre existence because you didn't plan ahead. How many regrets will you have then?

Often, our desire to give ourselves pleasure now is an attempt to cover up for other more substantial things missing in our lives. Because we don't want to address those deeper needs, which are very difficult to face, we try to fill the holes with temporary plugs. If you remember, earlier on in the book, I talked about delaying eating that chocolate bar as a way of practising self-discipline. But it is not only an exercise in tormenting yourself. When you begin to bring more discipline into your mindset, it allows you to look deeper into those holes and see what exactly is buried there.

Delaying satisfaction means feeling dissatisfied now, which is a great time to look at why. If you demand to be satisfied instantaneously, think about how you feel when you are unable to experience that. Instead of following your impulses, make a choice and nurture the discipline to stick to your decisions, which may bring you greater rewards in the future. Over time, you can learn to improve your self-control and focus more on your long-term plans.

Here are some ways for you to practise delayed gratification:

1. Practise mindfulness, which will give you insight into why you want something and what emotions you are experiencing at the thought of not being able to have it now. Learn to rewire your behavioral impulses and reach a more relaxed state.

2. Monitor your trigger distractions, such as your cell phone or TV. You can even use one of the many apps which monitor your self-use and lock you out of your internet for a time that you set yourself. Once you use these, you will realize just how reliant you are on this kind of stimulation, which is the first step to breaking that habit of instant gratification.

3. Love soft, fizzy drinks? Yeah, me too, but I never buy them because I can't resist the temptation to drink too much of them. Considering the amount of sugar that is in them, plus who knows what else, I purposefully avoid buying them when at the supermarket so I am not making life hard for myself. It's much easier to avoid unhealthy junk food when it's not sitting in your fridge.

4. The next time you feel upset, try to deal with those emotions instead of reaching for a glass of something alcoholic, or a cigarette. Handling your emotions without a crutch will become easier over time, and you will be in a better position to make more rational decisions.

5. If you can't avoid the idea of rewards, make sure that it is in response to avoiding something that isn't good for you. For example, if you manage to refrain from playing online games for a week, reward yourself at the end of it with a treat, such as an evening out or a massage at a health spa.

6. Give yourself a pep talk and discover how a positive voice can outweigh negative emotions. Self-dialogue is used by many successful people when faced with challenges and if you get used to doing so, you will notice how you can rewire your brain to find solutions instead of problems.

A word of warning – delaying gratification can take a lot of effort and it is much easier to give in to your impulses. But creating strategies to deal with your impulses in favor of future rewards is a skill that you can learn if you wish to do so. Spend more time focusing on your inner needs and less on superficial fixes and you will get there eventually.

CONCLUSION

It can be very difficult to learn how to be emotionally intelligent.

As you will have discovered throughout this book, we are very complex beings with complicated lives and it's not easy to apply everything that you have read here overnight. You have your own background, upbringing, personality, character, likes, dislikes, dreams, problems and expectations.

You are unique, and any attempt to fit you into a general framework of behaviour would be impossible to do. Only you know your own life story, your strengths and weaknesses, and your goals. The only assumption I can make is that if you have read this book, it is because you are curious about finding ways of improving your life in some way. That is something that we can all do on a daily basis with small steps.

Emotional intelligence is just one of the topics that have become popular in recent years and the tips and techniques that you will have come across in this book are the result of heaps of research that has been carried out by specialists in their field. As neuroscientists, psychologists, and psychiatrists learn more about the human condition, a school of thought has evolved in positive psychology that refers to emotional intelligence as a means to greatly improve your wellbeing. It has also been recognised by companies for its importance within the work environment. Those aspiring to be good leaders are adopting the skills of emotional intelligence to inspire and create stronger, more successful teams. More value is being placed by recruiters on those who are seen as a 'people person', and if you exhibit these aptitudes, you have a better chance than others of securing a job or even being promoted.

Emotional intelligence is a multifaceted discipline that is also being used to help people overcome common problems such as anxiety, depression and stress-related illnesses. There has been a steady rise recently in the interest in mindfulness-based programs (MBPs) such as Mindfulness-Based Stress Reduction (MBSR) and Mindfulness-Based Cognitive Therapy. This has filtered through to healthcare, education, as well as the mainstream culture. The emphasis is on recognizing the causes of human distress and offering ways to relieve them. The approach is simple: present moment focus, decentering and focussing on developing qualities such as joy, compassion and more behavioral self-regulation.

The University of Oxford Department of Psychiatry has actually set up a clinical centre to help in the prevention of depression and mental illness using well-researched mindfulness techniques. Depression is a common disorder that can be totally debilitating to the sufferer, and Mindfulness-Based Cognitive Therapy (MBCT) has been developed to help those at risk. Controlled trials have shown that it is an effective approach to preventing depressive relapse over 60 weeks of follow up and is an alternative to long-term antidepressant use.

The primary research has focussed on prevention and helping people to learn skills that develop resilience and reduce the chance of depression occurring. MBCT can also be applied to a range of other conditions, such as people who feel suicidal, suffer from health anxiety or who have cardiovascular disease, as well as helping people through transitional stages of their lives.

Clearly, these advances promise to offer help to many people and it is hoped by centres like the one above that MBCT will eventually be incorporated fully into the national health system. Imagine that: going to the doctor for some mindfulness help, not as an alternative type of mumbo-jumbo therapy but as a bona fide part of the health treatment on offer. The goal is this: a world without depression, where people live with understanding, compassion and responsiveness.

I've talked a lot in this book about getting in touch with your inner emotions – observing them, reflecting on them and thinking about ways to be more aware of your actions. It's a process which requires time, patience and motivation. When you feel angry, usually you feel justified in your response – someone did something to cause that reaction in you or something happened. Sure, it makes sense, and we are all affected by external influences daily. If emotional intelligence is about being aware of this, then mindfulness is one way to access possible outcomes, rather than being carried away by negative thoughts and feelings.

As science advances, it's worth pointing out that we are now beginning to get a much better understanding of how mindfulness and even meditation can influence our responses by actually rewiring our neural functioning. This affects our hormones, neurotransmitters and overall psychology – it relates to how we feel. The brain is a finely-tuned engine that is responsible for monitoring our internal world, which eventually spills out into the external. If you receive some bad news, the negative sensation you experience is going to be obvious to the next person you talk to. That's because we naturally communicate how we feel, without stopping to think about how it will come across and influence others.

Recent brain research

So what are the current science bods saying about how we can impact our brain circuitry to elevate positive experiences? Is it possible to shift the neurocircuitry to enhance our emotional intelligence?

With the advancement of neuroimaging during a brain scan, we can see a lot about how it works. Methods such as computerized tomography (CT), positron emission tomography (PET), magnetic resonance imaging (MRI) and regional cerebral blood flow (rCBF) are all ways in which we can gain a greater understanding of what is going on inside the brain.

The prefrontal cortex can be found in the frontal lobe, just where your forehead is. This is the decision-making area and is also responsible for regulating emotions and processing pain. Amazingly, many of the findings related to mindfulness and meditation practice have been observed here. The average cortical thickness of those with 40-50 years of meditation under their belt measured the same as the thickness of 20-year-olds, showing that meditation may be useful in slowing down neural degeneration.

Other research has shown that 8 weeks of mindfulness-oriented focused meditation increased activity in the dorsolateral prefrontal cortex, which is involved in holding and monitoring attention.

The insula region is a mysterious structure of the brain that sits between the frontal and temporal lobes. It is here that emotion, arousal and awareness are thought to exist and studies have found that certain disorders have a deficiency of introspective awareness, but mindfulness works to restore this balance. Anterior insula activation was seen to be less by those engaged in long-term meditation, signifying they weren't affected by distress in others but increased in compassion. This is the triumph of reason over emotion.

We've mentioned the amygdala earlier on in the book, which is the powerhouse of our fear and anxiety, often preventing us from attaining a sense of achievement and wellbeing. It's interesting to note that one study showed how breath awareness decreased activity in the amygdala, so the old adage, "Take a deep breath" really does have its uses. When we focus on our breath, we regain control of our emotions, which may want to go haywire. Not only that, mindfulness and meditation have been seen to influence the functional activity of the amygdala, decreasing the overall volume of fear-processing.

The hippocampus is a horseshoe area mostly associated with memory and also plays its part in regulating neuroendocrine functions and emotional behavior such as depression and anxiety. Studies show that the response of those with mild cognitive impairment who undertake a period of mindfulness and meditation exhibited a reduction in hippocampal volume atrophy. This has great implications for conditions such as Alzheimer's. Meditation has also been seen to increase grey matter volume, reducing neurodegenerative disease and some of the complications of aging.

Neurotransmitters and hormones are both influenced by mindfulness and meditation practices and the secretion of the two shifts our experience of the world around us. The brain activates these mechanisms in times of stress, sending a signal to the amygdala to release neurotransmitters like noradrenaline, glutamate, and serotonin. Meanwhile, the hypothalamus releases corticotropin hormones that bind to receptors of the anterior pituitary gland, responsible for the secretion of cortisol. Meditation and mindfulness certainly play their part when we are faced with anxiety, stress and fear because they focus on calming all of the brain activity related to that internal chemical warfare going on.

These are pretty big claims and although a lot of the research being carried out is still cutting-edge, the more advanced technology and neuroimaging gets, the clearer an idea we will have of how mindfulness and meditation can play their part in emotional intelligence. We are actually talking about how to control the negative aspects of our thought processes on the brain, molding it to be healthier, more responsive and better able to help us maintain calm and inner peace. That's not a bad goal to have!

Perhaps this is just one of the ways how you can develop a new you. If you can enhance the neural passages and hormones in the brain, effectively you are creating a new, better you. It is like a neural auto-correction system, similar to what you can find on any computer program. Each time you type in a mistake that could distort your whole word or sentence, auto-correct kicks in and rectifies it. A lot of auto-correct software also gives you the choice of leaving your error as it is or offers suggestions. Imagine that is how we can control our responses and emotions – now, that is real power, isn't it?

Please take on board the steps that I have introduced in this book as much as you can.

If you are able to strip away the layers that you have built up over the years that define how you feel, respond, react, and deal with challenges and conflicts, may I suggest that you aim for the following:

- More self-love
- More confidence in your abilities
- More focus on the present
- More curiosity about life
- More enthusiasm to try new things
- More love and compassion for others

You can do it.

This book offers you all the tools that you need to take a few steps back, to pause and to reflect on what it is that you feel is missing, and how to attain your goals.

- By learning how to understand those things called emotions and to recognize that by becoming more emotionally savvy you can get more out of life, you can embark on a new journey.
- By acquiring better self-awareness, you can focus on your potential and help reduce conflict, strengthen your relationships and even create fruitful new ones.
- By raising your self-esteem and improving self-discipline, you will discover new opportunities waiting for you all you have to do is pursue them.
- By recognizing your failures, you are on the road to blazing new trails with the power of hindsight and experience.
- By dealing with the past and living in the present, you will discover a new paradigm of contentment and fulfillment.
- By overcoming negative emotions such as anger, you will find a new, liberated way of being that is not dependent on the actions of others.
- By being kinder to yourself, you will overcome doubts and fears and see a new you in the mirror.
- By having more empathy with others, you can open up new lines of deeper human connection.

- By slowing down your thoughts and your breath, you will be able to focus on what is important and form new pacts with yourself.
- By taking care of your mind and body, you will create a new sense of wellbeing and vitality.
- By practising patience, you will learn how to appreciate new experiences in life and be more excited about the future.

When you have found this balance, you will have achieved a new you.

I hope you begin today!

—

If you've benefited from my book, please take some time to leave a review on Amazon. Thank you!

EXERCISES FOR
EMOTIONAL INTELLIGENCE

Here are further exercises to guide you through the subject of emotional intelligence. They will be useful in helping you to reflect on yourself at this current moment. Feel free to try them again in a few weeks or months as you go through the process of building a new you to see what progress you are making.

You will also find an example of a Positivity Journal that you can use to record how you feel each day, or you can even keep a daily journal of your own in a notebook. At the end, you will find an introduction to basic meditation and mindfulness practises, which may help you to take time out, feel more grounded and allow you to reconnect with yourself.

Enjoy and good luck!

For a PDF version of these exercises, please visit www.bit.ly/pdfeib

EXERCISE 1

How emotionally intelligent are you?

Answer the questions as honestly as you can. There are no correct or incorrect answers here, just pointers for you to reflect on once you have completed the questionnaire.

1. I become defensive easily when criticized.

| Strongly Disagree | Disagree | Neither Agree Nor Disagree | Agree | Strongly Agree |

2. I remain calm under pressure.

| Strongly Disagree | Disagree | Neither Agree Nor Disagree | Agree | Strongly Agree |

3. I can handle setbacks easily.

| Strongly Disagree | Disagree | Neither Agree Nor Disagree | Agree | Strongly Agree |

4. I manage anger, stress, anxiety when facing challenges.

| Strongly Disagree | Disagree | Neither Agree Nor Disagree | Agree | Strongly Agree |

5. I use criticism and feedback to improve.

| Strongly Disagree | Disagree | Neither Agree Nor Disagree | Agree | Strongly Agree |

6. I am a positive person.

| Strongly Disagree | Disagree | Neither Agree Nor Disagree | Agree | Strongly Agree |

7. I have a good sense of humor.

| Strongly Disagree | Disagree | Neither Agree Nor Disagree | Agree | Strongly Agree |

8. I try to see the other person's point of view.

| Strongly Disagree | Disagree | Neither Agree Nor Disagree | Agree | Strongly Agree |

9. I am aware that my behavior affects others.

| Strongly Disagree | Disagree | Neither Agree Nor Disagree | Agree | Strongly Agree |

10. I air my grievances with tact.

Strongly   Neither Agree   Strongly
Disagree   Disagree   Nor Disagree   Agree   Agree

11. I listen without making judgements about the other person.

Strongly   Neither Agree   Strongly
Disagree   Disagree   Nor Disagree   Agree   Agree

12. I admit it when I make a mistake.

Strongly   Neither Agree   Strongly
Disagree   Disagree   Nor Disagree   Agree   Agree

13. Now, ask someone who knows you very well to also answer the above questions on your behalf. The results may surprise you and even push you to reassert the opinion of how others see you. What can you improve on or change?

EXERCISE 2

<u>Self-management</u>

Grade yourself from 1 to 5 on the following and then add up your total.

1 = Almost Never   2 = Rarely   3 = Sometimes
4 = Usually   5 = Almost always

I can stay calm, even in difficult circumstances:
1   2   3   4   5

I don't have outbursts of rage:
1   2   3   4   5

I feel happy:
1   2   3   4   5

I'm not irritated by other people or things:
1   2   3   4   5

I don't get carried away and do things I regret afterwards:
1   2   3   4   5

<u>Your results</u>
14-25 = This is an area of strength for you
7-13 = Pay some attention to the aspects of this area you feel are weakest in
0-6 = This is an area you need to focus on developing

Emotional Self-Management is the ability to manage your emotions, stay focussed and to take responsibility for your actions without making rash decisions

EXERCISE 3

Motivation

Grade yourself from 1 to 5 on the following and then add up your total.

1 = Almost Never   2 = Rarely   3 = Sometimes
4 = Usually   5 = Almost always

I am clear about my goals for the future:
1   2   3   4   5

My career is moving in the right direction:
1   2   3   4   5

I remain enthusiastic even when I encounter setbacks:
1   2   3   4   5

I feel excited when I think of my goals:
1   2   3   4   5

I act consistently to move towards my goals:
1   2   3   4   5

Your results

14-25 = You have strong self-motivation

7-13 = Think of the areas that you can improve on to increase your discipline

0-6 = Reassess your goals and work harder to achieve them

Motivation is the ability to move towards your goals using self-discipline and persevering when facing obstacles or setbacks.

EXERCISE 4

Empathy

Grade yourself from 1 to 5 on the following and then add up your total.

1 = Almost Never   2 = Rarely   3 = Sometimes
4 = Usually   5 = Almost always

My colleagues are very communicative:
1   2   3   4   5

I get on well with all of my work colleagues:
1   2   3   4   5

I find it easy to "read" other people's emotions:
1   2   3   4   5

I can predict how my colleagues feel in any given situation:
1   2   3   4   5

People prefer to work with me rather than equally talented colleagues:
1   2   3   4   5

Your results

14-25 = You have a strong sense of empathy

7-13 = You need to consider how to improve your communication with others

0-6 = Try to improve your people skills to achieve more empathy

Empathy is the ability to understand and respond appropriately to what other people are feeling. This requires self-awareness and good communication skills.

EXERCISE 5

Relationship management

Grade yourself from 1 to 5 on the following and then add up your total.

1 = Almost Never   2 = Rarely   3 = Sometimes
4 = Usually   5 = Almost always

I find it easy to get on with other people:
1   2   3   4   5

I can strike up a conversation with anyone:
1   2   3   4   5

I don't mind losing an argument:
1   2   3   4   5

I feel moved when other people get emotional:
1   2   3   4   5

I have a lot of patience for incompetent people:
1   2   3   4   5

Your results

14-25 = You manage relationships very effectively

7-13 = You need to consider how to improve your communication with others

0-6 = Improve your people skills to better your relationship management

Relationship Management is the ability to handle emotions in relationships and to be able to influence and inspire others. It is an essential skill for successful teamwork and leadership.

EXERCISE 6

Positivity journal

Keep a record of 3 positive experiences each day for 7 days.

Reflect on your day before you go to sleep each night and identify at least 3 positive things that happened. The positive experience can be something simple or more complex, as long as it is positive.

This positive reflection will train your brain to continue to acknowledge the positive aspects of your life and prevent you from focussing only on the negatives. After the first week, keep going and see how much better you get at facing challenges, anxiety and fears.

Day one

1..

2..

3..

Day two

1..

2..

3..

Day three

1..

2..

3..

Day four

1...

2...

3...

Day five

1...

2...

3...

Day six

1...

2...

3...

Day seven

1...

2...

3...

EXERCISE 7

A meditation exercise

1. Choose a quiet time of day when you can be alone or undisturbed.

2. Turn off your TV, any music, and smartphone or disable any notifications.

3. Sit on a comfortable straight-backed chair or cross-legged on the floor if you prefer.

4. Close your eyes and relax.

5. Begin by focussing on your breathing and feel the sensation of air flowing into your nostrils and out of your mouth.

6. Breathe in, following your breath as you do so and count to 4.

7. Hold your breath for a count of 7.

8. Breathe out slowly, counting to 8.

9. Inhale again and exhale again, following your breath as your belly rises and falls and the air passes through it.

10. Once you've narrowed your concentration on your breath, begin to widen your focus. Become aware of sounds, sensations, and thoughts.

11. Embrace each thought or sensation without judging it as good or bad. If your mind starts to race, return your focus to your breathing.

12. Sit calmly for 5 minutes before you open your eyes.

Most people find that it takes at least 20 minutes for the mind to begin to settle, so don't worry if you find it difficult at first. Practise once a day at a regular time for 30 minutes and see what a difference it makes to your overall wellbeing.

EXERCISE 8

<u>Mindfulness exercise</u>

Whether you are driving, eating, walking or home-decorating, being mindful can help you to focus with more clarity and learn to appreciate the present moment. Start by bringing your attention to the sensations in your body.

1. Breathe in through your nose and allow the air to fill your lungs. Then breathe out slowly through your mouth. This pattern can slow down your heart rate and lower your blood pressure, helping you relax.

2. Proceed with what you are doing slowly and with full deliberation.

3. Engage your senses and notice every touch, smell, sound and sight.

4. If your mind wanders, gently bring your attention back to the sensations you are experiencing around you.

5. Notice your thoughts but just let them pass and concentrate on being in the moment.

APPENDIX

<u>References</u>

Yale Center for Emotional Intelligence

Emotional Intelligence: Why It Can Matter More Than IQ
Daniel Goleman, 2012

Emotional Intelligence
Peter Salovey, John D. Mayer, 1990

The differential effects of general mental ability and emotional intelligence on academic performance and social interactions
L.J. Song, G.-H. Huang, K.Z. Peng, K.S. Law, C.-S. Wong, Zhijun Chen, 2010

Increasing emotional intelligence: (How) is it possible?
Delphine Nelis, Jordi Quoidbach, M. Mikolajczak, Michel Hansenne, 2009

Do schools kill creativity? TED.com
Sir Ken Robinson, 2007

Rhetoric (The Complete Three Books)
Aristotle, Simon & Brown, 2018

The circumplex as a general model of the structure of emotions and personality.
Plutchik, Robert (1997)

American-Japanese cultural differences in intensity ratings of facial expressions of emotion
David Matsumoto & Paul Ekman, 1989

Varieties of reported emotional experience
Alan S. Cowen, Dacher Keltner, Proceedings of the National Academy of Sciences 2017

Children's Perceptions of Self-Esteem
Jessica Koltz, 2018

Dove Self-Esteem Fund, 2008

Can you become addicted to chocolate, Harvard Health Publishing
Michael Craig Miller, M.D., 2013

Reuters.com
I Am Bolt, 2016

Mindset: The New Psychology of Success
Carol S. Dweck, Random house, 2006

A meta-analytical review of brain activity associated with intertemporal decisions:
Evidence for an anterior-posterior tangibility axis
Benjamin James Smith, 2018

Physiological and psychological correlates of forgiveness
Kevin Seybold, 2001

A review of forgiveness process models and a coping framework to guide future
research
Peter Strelan, 2006

The Relation of Social Isolation, Loneliness, and Social Support to Disease
Outcomes Among the Elderly
Joe Tomaka, Sharon Thompson, Rebecca Palacios, 2006

Does positive affect influence health?
Pressman, Sarah D. Cohen, Sheldon, 2005

Neural correlates of attentional expertise in long-term meditation practitioners
J. A. Brefczynski-Lewis, A. Lutz, H. S. Schaefer, D. B. Levinson, and R. J. Davidson,
2007

Attention in Delay of Gratification.
W. Mischel, E. Ebbesen, 1970

Delay of Gratification: Impulsive Choices and Problem Behaviors in Early and
Late Adolescence

Edelgard Wulfert, Jennifer A. Block, Elizabeth Santa Ana, Monica L. Rodriguez, Melissa Colsman, 2002

University of Oxford Mindfulness Research Centre

Meditation experience is associated with increased cortical thickness
Sara W. Lazar et al., 2005

Mindfulness training induces structural connectome changes in insula networks
Paul B. Sharp, 2018
Mindfulness meditation regulates anterior insula activity during empathy for social pain
Davide Laneri, 2017

Quantitative EEG, Event-Related Potentials and Neurotherapy
Juri D.Kropotov, 2009

Mindful attention to breath regulates emotions via increased amygdala–prefrontal cortex connectivity
Anselm Doll et al., 2016

Meditation and yoga practice are associated with smaller right amygdala volume: the Rotterdam study Rinske A. Gotink et al., 2018

Reduced interference in working memory following mindfulness training is associated with increases in hippocampal volume
Jonathan Greenberg, 2018

Procrastination and Stress Exploring the Role of Self-compassion
Fuschia M Sirois, 2014

www.ingramcontent.com/pod-product-compliance
Lightning Source LLC
Chambersburg PA
CBHW020909080526
44589CB00011B/517